Shakespeare
*the dark comedies
to the last plays*

Shakespeare

the dark comedies to the last
plays: from satire to celebration

R. A. Foakes

The University Press of Virginia
Charlottesville

The University Press of Virginia
Copyright © R. A. Foakes 1971

First Published 1971

Standard Book Number: 8139-0327-0
Library of Congress Catalog Card Number: 70-146536

Printed in Great Britain

Contents

Preface

This study falls into three sections, but is concerned primarily with Shakespeare's development towards and achievement in his last plays. The middle section, on satire and tragedy, provides a bridge between the other two, and is limited in scope to what is essential to the argument. This part could have been developed at much greater length, and I have considered some of the issues raised in it elsewhere, especially in an essay, 'Tragedy at the Children's Theatres after 1600: A Challenge to the Adult Stage', printed in *The Elizabethan Theatre II*, edited by David Galloway (1970), pp. 37–59.

It would be impossible to record all influences on me, and all my debts, and in the course of the book I have referred only to what is immediately relevant. I would, however, like to express my gratitude to Paula Neuss and to Michael Hattaway who helped me greatly with their advice.

I am grateful to Messrs Faber & Faber Ltd and to Random House Inc., New York for permission to quote 'Musée des Beaux Arts' from W. H. Auden, *Collected Shorter Poems 1927–1957*.

R. A. F.

1
Introduction

Some years ago, when I was editing *King Henry VIII*, I was inclined to accept the conventional treatment of Shakespeare's last plays as 'myths or symbolic patterns',[1] and to assume that in spite of their acknowledged complexity as dramatic poems, they were inferior plays for the stage, 'the most depersonalized' of Shakespeare's plays, and 'the most difficult to bring to life in the theatre'.[2] Much of the growing body of criticism of these plays has encouraged, and still fosters, such a view, for there is no doubt that its main concern has been with the 'significance' of the plays; so an examination of the response to these plays in the present century has shown that:[3]

> By far the biggest and most influential school of criticism we have to consider is a school of many sects. Its members are united in the belief that the Romances are written in a form of other-speaking, and must be translated before their significance can be understood. There is little point at this stage in the waning of the century in speaking once more of the tremendous impact of anthropology and comparative religion on criticism, but it must be said that interest in the last plays would have

[1] The phrase is from Philip Edwards, 'Shakespeare's Romances: 1900-1957', *Shakespeare Survey*, 11 (1958), p. 14.
[2] See my Introduction to the New Arden edition of *King Henry VIII* (1957), p. xli.
[3] Edwards, *loc. cit.*, p. 6.

1

been a shadow of what it has been in fact, if vegetation rites
and royal deaths and resurrections, and the symbolic patterns
in which the inner realities of human experience display themselves, had been less enthusiastically received into the small-talk
of the age.

A stress on ideas and themes tends to lead our attention away
from the plays as drama; and much criticism of them is written
as if it were commenting on the ideas in a rather difficult novel,
or describing a pattern of symbols.

Certainly the abundant commentary of recent years has taught
us much about the richness and complexity of the poetry and
themes in these plays, and it would be absurd to neglect such
matters in discussing *Cymbeline* or *The Tempest*. At the same
time, we ought to consider whether it is not equally absurd to
neglect the nature of the dramatic action, and the shape these
plays take in the two or three hours' traffic of the stage.

For to consider them as dramatic structures is to encounter
at once a number of difficulties and problems that may be
ignored or sidestepped in a consideration of the plays as vehicles
of ideas. So, for example, the interchange in Act IV of *The
Winter's Tale* between Polixenes and Perdita on art and nature
looms large in most interpretations of the play, although it
occupies perhaps half a minute of stage-time in a long and busy
scene, full of spectacle and song, and may pass little noticed by
an audience. In the theatre, by contrast, Autolycus makes an
enormous impact in this scene, as elsewhere in the later part
of the play, and yet in many accounts of it, 'there has been
silence about him'.[1] To consider the play in terms of its dramatic
structure rather than its thematic patterns is necessarily to be
concerned with the function of Autolycus at least as much as
with the relation of art and nature – and a study of the role of
Autolycus may prove to throw light on this relation too.

The difficulties offered by *Cymbeline* have seemed to many
to be weaknesses in the play, and the clever attempts by D. A.
Traversi and others to read the play in consistent symbolic
terms have not satisfied everyone. So a recent editor, supporting
a view of the play as unsatisfactory, cited as still the best

[1] Charles R. Crow, 'Chiding the Plays: Then till Now', *Shakespeare Survey*, 18
(1965), p. 8. See below, p. 137, n. 3.

account of it the essay by Harley Granville-Barker in which he complained about various faults in it, notably an inconsistency of characterization in speeches of Imogen, Posthumus and Cloten, which seem not to belong to the character and mark what he called 'sheer lapses from dramatic integrity'.[1] These characters, he felt, simply do not always behave or speak in the way Shakespearean characters, conceived as consistent wholes, ought to speak. Granville-Barker observed accurately, but supposed that someone other than Shakespeare had a hand in the play, for he could only judge *Cymbeline* in terms of expectations derived from earlier plays, the central tragedies for example, and was looking for consistency of character in psychological and linguistic terms. He was trapped, that is to say, in traditional categories, conventional ways of thinking about Shakespeare, and did not see that the inconsistencies in *Cymbeline* could be explained as a new development in Shakespeare's technique. It is part of the argument of this book that, beginning with the dark comedies, Shakespeare learned how to liberate himself from a commitment to characters presented with psychological and linguistic consistency, in order to achieve special kinds of effects in his later plays, and particularly as one means of distancing his audience from the characters and preventing identification with them, in the way an audience identifies with Hamlet. What has seemed clumsy to many readers of *Cymbeline* may be merely a daring new development in Shakespeare's dramatic art.

The Winter's Tale is often presented to us as a great play in terms of its symbolic consistency, but at the expense of Autolycus; *Cymbeline* is usually presented to us as a failure, because it is hard to read in a consistent symbolic way and does not offer consistent characters or speech. Yet no one disputes that as Granville-Barker said, Shakespeare was, by the time he wrote these, a 'past-master of his craft',[2] who was not likely to make elementary dramatic mistakes. To see these plays in the theatre is to realize how splendidly they work on the stage, and how little connection there is between much conventional

---

[1] Harley Granville-Barker, *Prefaces to Shakespeare*, Second Series (1930), pp. 237-8, 290. The recent editor is J. C. Maxwell, in the New Cambridge edition (1960), p. xxxii.

[2] *Ibid.*, p. 238.

criticism and the play as experienced by an audience. For an audience, in my experience, sees Autolycus as a prominent and important figure, and finds itself little troubled by the inconsistencies and other 'weaknesses' noted by many critics in *Cymbeline*.

This book springs from an attempt to understand and explain the last plays as structures designed for performance. In order to do this, it has proved necessary to start from the dark comedies, and to say something about the innovations in the theatre in the early years of the seventeenth century, in particular the growth of satiric drama at that time, for in his development as a dramatist after 1600, Shakespeare seems to have been much influenced by, and to have developed in his own way, new techniques and possibilities for drama that arose particularly in connection with the revival of the children's companies. In relation to the plays John Marston, Ben Jonson, Chapman, Middleton and others were writing for the Children at St Paul's and Blackfriars, Shakespeare's heroic tragedies, like *Hamlet* and *Othello*, look almost old-fashioned in their conventional assumptions. Shakespeare's most experimental plays at this time were the dark comedies, and the main line of development of his dramatic skills lay from these through the late tragedies like *Coriolanus* and *Antony and Cleopatra* to the last plays.

In presenting this argument I have tried to pare it down to essentials in the interests of clarity and to resist the inevitable temptation in discussing Shakespeare's plays to comment on all aspects of them. At the same time, it leads necessarily into a consideration of the meanings of the plays, those meanings shaped and revealed by the unfolding dramatic action. In this way, the argument tends to return to themes and ideas, especially in relation to *The Tempest*, which is in some ways the most complex of Shakespeare's dramas. However, this is to arrive at, or put stress on, a rather different body of meanings from those commonly emphasized in treatments of the plays as literary texts, and with reference to their mythic, symbolic, philosophical or doctrinal implications. Studies of this kind tend to lose sight of the life of the drama and to deal in abstractions; and they need to be supplemented, modified and, in their wilder extravagances, corrected or rejected by another kind of approach, which begins from the dramatic action and which takes this as a controlling perspective, however far the discussion may be led from time to time into other areas of exploration.

In what follows I try to develop such an approach,[1] and my starting-point is the dramatic shaping of the action, or what I sometimes call the tonality of the play, the pattern of expectations established by the sum of relations existing between the parts of the action at any given point. I say 'at any given point', because to consider the dramatic shape of a play is necessarily to emphasize its nature as a process taking place in time. The relation of the parts of the action to one another, the reasons for the presentation of events in a particular sequence or for the introduction of a particular character, can be crucial for an understanding of the way a play works as drama. These things may seem simple enough, but they raise complicated and difficult questions, questions often ignored in critical commentaries, or left, so to speak, asleep. So, for example, in *Measure for Measure*, it is easy to dwell on the powerfully realized scenes involving Angelo and Isabella, and their mutual 'temptation' of one another:

> Is this her fault or mine?
> The tempter or the tempted, who sins most?

> (II.ii.162)

The urgency and richness of the verse in this scene, which are of course appropriate to its mood, attract commentary, and the relation of Angelo and Isabella is very important; but it is

[1] I do not claim that the argument I present is entirely new; indeed, the ground for it has been prepared by a number of critics, most notably by Anne Righter in a general way; by O. J. Campbell in relation to the dark comedies; by A. Caputi and G. K. Hunter in relation to satire and the plays of Marston; by Harley Granville-Barker; by S. L. Bethell in the brilliant early chapters of his book on *The Winter's Tale* (1947), and F. R. Leavis in his essay in *Scrutiny*, X (1941-2), all in relation to the last plays. More recently, Norman Rabkin, in *Shakespeare and the Common Understanding* 1967, a book that became available to me only after I had completed my own, has taken account of the 'ostentatious theatricality' of the last plays in a fine essay that nevertheless moves towards abstract ideas and is not, in the end, much concerned with the dramatic shaping of the plays. (See my note below, p. 98.) All these and more have pointed the way, but no one, I believe, has pursued the implications of an analysis of these plays beginning from dramatic structure and tonality; and the extent to which such an analysis challenges critical orthodoxies may be seen by glancing at the introductions to the Arden editions or at the essays reprinted in the collections of 'views' and 'casebooks' which have proliferated in recent years.

important also to observe that the tonality of the action here is established in part by the long scene we have just witnessed of the trial of Pompey Bum and Froth, with its bawdy good humour and vitality. We need to ask why Shakespeare displayed at length this comic trial, but not that of Claudio, and what effect it has on the subsequent action.

This study is much concerned with questions of this kind, such as why Barnardine was introduced into this play or what the function is of the long masque in *The Tempest* (that 'vanity', as Prospero calls it). For problems such as these are continually raised by a study of dramatic structure and tonality in the plays. Most attention here is given to the last plays, except for *Pericles*. I have not dealt with this play for several reasons. It survives only in a bad text, which alone makes it a difficult play to assess. Technically, the use of Gower as a chorus to frame and distance the action is an innovation, and the play has some brilliant episodes, which have produced sympathetic accounts of its occasional power and a notable poem in T. S. Eliot's 'Marina'. At the same time, regarded from the viewpoint of dramatic artistry, it remains a simple play, lacking a clear structure beyond its portrayal of a sequence of events illustrating, for the most part, the truth of Pericles' words:

> . . . I see that Time's the King of men;
> He's both their parent, and he is their grave,
> And gives them what he will, not what they crave.

> (II.iii.45)

It is true that Pericles is united with Marina in a moving scene at the end of the play, when 'the holy gods' seem to intervene, but this union does not arise in any necessary way out of the action we have witnessed; it appears rather as the latest of Time's whims, and in this, the first of the 'romances', Shakespeare did not, as far as we can tell, succeed in solving what was a problem for him in other late plays, how to create simultaneously a sense of dramatic necessity in the action and a sense that the characters are not in control of their affairs, which are governed rather by chance or providence. However, this needs to be argued, and the argument begins in the following pages, from the dark comedies.

2

Shakespeare
and satirical comedy

(i) *All's Well that Ends Well*

Of the three 'problem comedies', *All's Well that Ends Well* has
seemed to commentators the most confused, and least satisfactory as a play. Few, perhaps, have had the opportunity of
seeing it performed, for until recent years it was rarely produced.
What a stage performance reveals is the degree to which the
tonality of the play is governed by the presence of figures like
Lavache and Parolles, who persuade us immediately that we
are in a comic world. It is true that the play begins from two
deaths, and brings on everyone in black, mourning for the death
of Bertram's father, in the first scene. Not only has the Count
Rossilion just died, but it appears that Helena has recently lost
a father too. But the mourning is all in show, in the appearance
of black costumes, and the first scene puts an end to it. The
death of his father liberates Bertram from the restrictions of
home and enables him to go to the court as ward of the King.
The death of her father frees Helena also, and allows her to
pursue her own designs.

What the scene brings home to us is the great convenience
for budding heroes and heroines in comedy of having parents
out of the way.[1] So Bertram's thoughts are all on the French

[1] The Countess, it is true, offers herself as a 'mother' to Helena in I.iii, but her
design, as she reveals it in the course of this scene, is to become her mother-in-law,
and help her to win Bertram as husband.

court, if we can trust Parolles, and Bertram's own few speeches
in the opening scene; and Helena, once left alone, confesses:

> I think not on my father,
> And these great tears grace his remembrance more
> Than those I shed for him. What was he like?
> I have forgot him.
>
> (I.i.73)

Her thoughts are all on love. Far from meditating on death,
she is found by Parolles in the contemplation of virginity.
Parolles, whom she, and through her we, know already to be
'a great way fool, solely a coward' (I.i.95), advises her to get
rid of her virginity as quickly as possible:

> *Parolles*   Virginity breeds mites, much like a cheese; consumes
> itself to the very paring, and so dies with feeding his
> own stomach. Besides, virginity is peevish, proud,
> idle, made of self-love, which is the most inhibited
> sin in the canon. Keep it not; you cannot choose but
> lose by it. Out with't. Within ten year it will make
> itself ten, which is a goodly increase, and the principal
> itself not much the worse. Away with't.
>
> *Helena*   How might one do, sir, to lose it to her own liking?
>
> (I.i.130)

Instead of objecting to his strain of bawdy conversation,
Helena is already considering how to lose her virginity to her
own liking. She is not so much answering him, as continuing a
meditation on 'that bright particular star' (l. 80) she loves, or
worships rather, Bertram. Parolles' bawdy nevertheless feeds
her imagination, as she broods on the image she has made of
Bertram as godlike, with his 'arched brows, his hawking eye,
his curls'. She has made of him an image of perfection, built
out of his appearance entirely, and worships at that shrine:

> heart too capable
> Of every line and trick of his sweet favour.
> But now he's gone, and my idolatrous fancy
> Must sanctify his relics.
>
> (I.i.89)

At the same time, she is determined to have him, never pausing
to notice the possible difference between her image of him and

what he is, and undeterred by his remoteness from her in rank. The distance between them, which she inflates in her mind, seems rather to be a challenge, and as she listens to Parolles, she thinks only of herself and Bertram, scheming how to bring it off. He ends by advising her to 'Get thee a good husband' (l. 200), words which she does not acknowledge directly, but which act as a cue to her in settling on her course of action. If she can but reach the court and cure the King's disease, it may prove the way to Bertram's love:

> Our remedies oft in ourselves do lie.
> Which we ascribe to Heaven. The fated sky
> Gives us free scope. Only doth backward pull
> Our slow designs when we ourselves are dull.
>
> (I.i.202)

This is Helena's theme, that the heavens may help those who help themselves, and will hinder those who do not. So she takes her place at the centre of the action already by the end of the first scene, deciding the plot, so to speak, for herself.

Under pressure from the Countess, Helena confesses her love for Bertram, finding an unexpected ally in Bertram's mother. Again there appears in Helena's speeches that combination of idolatry and business-like determination to succeed. Bertram is imagined as the sun, inhabiting another sphere:

> Thus, Indian-like,
> Religious in mine error, I adore
> The sun, that looks upon his worshipper,
> But knows of him no more.
>
> (I.iii.195)

At the same time, Helena enlists the Countess's aid in venturing to the court, and admits that her sole motive in going there is the very practical one of losing her virginity to Bertram; her father, the great physician Gerard de Narbonne, has left to her the secret of remedies which may cure the King, but to achieve this cure would be a means, not an end:

> *Helena*   Amongst the rest
> There is a remedy approv'd, set down,
> To cure the desperate languishings whereof
> The King is render'd lost.

Countess	This was your motive
	For Paris, was it? Speak.
Helena	My lord your son made me to think of this,
	Else Paris, and the medicine, and the King
	Had from the conversation of my thoughts
	Haply been absent then.

(I.iii.218)

It is only now that Helena claims something more than her 'father's skill' in this mission, and appeals to 'the luckiest stars in Heaven', as if certain of their blessing.

Her encounter with the King in Act II grows out of what has passed, and must be seen in the light of that. At first he is incredulous of her powers, and rejects her offered help, although on his first appearance in I.ii he had wished her father alive: 'If he were living, I would try him yet'. Now he tries to brush her aside as a quack, but as she presses, and the conversation moves on, almost imperceptibly, with the King leading, they begin to talk in couplets, and the dialogue acquires a ritualistic, incantatory note, as Helena appeals to Heaven:

He that of greatest works is finisher
Oft does them by the weakest minister,

(II.i.135)

and again:

But most it is presumption in us when
The help of Heaven we count the act of men

(II.i.150)

Here she seems to reject her earlier position, 'Our remedies oft in ourselves do lie', but the rejection is more apparent than real. She tells the King in effect to believe she *may* be for this time the agent of Heaven; the remedy may lie in himself, if he will stop thinking of her as an 'empiric', and take her offered aid, which may, by God's grace, work on him:

Of Heaven, not me, make an experiment.

(II.i.153)

This does not make Helena 'divine', as some would have her,

or a 'medium', or 'miracle-worker';[1] it is rather that her combination of virtue, ambition, confidence in herself, and faith,
bring success, so that indeed for this act she happens to become
Heaven's agent. Dramatically, the sense of Heaven as instrumental is necessary to make credible the rapid recovery of the
King within a day from a disease that has defeated all his
physicians. Her success confirms Helena's skill and wisdom,
but she has not acted out of charity or saintliness, and is quick
to demand her fee:

> Then shalt thou give me with thy kingly hand
> What husband in thy power I will command.
>
> (II.i.192)

For this is no saint, but Helena, whose name echoes from
Helen of Troy, as Lafeu reminds us in this scene, when he
leaves her alone with the King, 'I am Cressid's uncle, That dare
leave two together' (I.ii.96). She is Helen with a difference, but
though she cannot, like her legendary namesake, turn all men's
heads, she has in common with her a very earthy devotion to
love.

For Helena, the cure of the King is a business deal, however
strong the appeal to Heaven in the scene, and however much the
matter may be published later as 'a showing of a Heavenly
Effect in an earthly Actor' (II.iii.23).   If the hand of Heaven
operates, it does so through a human agent who has her eye
firmly fixed on one object, the man she wants, and who makes
her demand at the first opportunity. The King summons the
five lords he can bestow, among them Bertram:

> This youthful parcel
> Of noble bachelors stand at my bestowing,
> O'er whom both sovereign power and father's voice
> I have to use. Thy frank election make.
> Thou hast power to choose, and they none to forsake.
>
> (II.iii.50)

They parade for inspection, like animals at a stud-farm, and
Helena looks them over one by one. The first four are ready to

---

[1] See, for example, G. Wilson Knight's essay, 'The Third Eye', in *The Sovereign
Flower* (1958), pp. 131-57, reprinted in Kenneth Muir (editor), *Shakespeare; The
Comedies* (Twentieth Century Views, 1965), pp. 133-51; and William B. Toole,
Shakespeare's Problem Plays (1966), p. 150.

B

have her, but she refuses them, while Lafeu, observing, supposes they refuse her; in fact only the last, Bertram, rejects her, because he knows her as a 'poor physician's daughter' (l. 113). The others value her for what she is, attractive, wise, virtuous; when Bertram says, 'I know her well', he does not really know her at all, but thinks only of her base birth. Even the King's promise to give her rank, honour and wealth cannot alter him, and though he must obey the royal command to marry her, it remains to him preposterous that he should be expected in a moment to change his opinion of her altogether:

> I find that she which late
> Was in my nobler thoughts most base, is now
> The praised of the King; who, so ennobled,
> Is as 'twere, born so
>
> (II.iii.168)

Bertram soon makes clear that he regards himself as 'Undone and forfeited to cares forever' (II.iii.260) by this marriage, and the speech quoted is spoken with some bitterness and irony by him. The implied questions and complaints are not unreasonable; why should he have to marry any girl the King happens to put his way? and how can he on a sudden so transform his view of things as to think her noble he has been accustomed to regard as base and a kind of servant? The questions do not compel an answer at this point, when the sympathy of the audience is all with Helena in her triumph. She has cured the King, and gained her immediate objective, marriage to Bertram. Since the other four lords would readily have taken her, it seems in many ways perverse of Bertram now to take counsel with Parolles, and go off to the wars, and he makes it worse by sending her back to his mother with the lie that "Twill be two days ere I shall see you' (II.iv.69).

At the same time, the achievements so far of Helena leave little doubt that she will succeed in her further aim, to lose her virginity to her liking. She pursues Bertram to the wars of Florence, and the story of how she contrives to substitute herself for the chaste Diana in bed with him, and so to fulfil the task he has imposed on her, of getting his ring and begetting his child, provides matter for the second half of the play. This is important in the action, but in a curious way subsidiary; Helena's final success is implicit in her attainment of a seemingly impossible marriage with one so 'above' her. Although her failure to lose her virginity provides in one aspect a calculated anti-climax, in another sense Helena has gained three parts of her aim; consummation is postponed, but inevitable, as the play's title indicates, and while it will exercise her ingenuity, and make for an exciting development of intrigues, it will simply demand the display by her of talents we already know she possesses.

If the first part of the play belongs to her, the last part belongs to Parolles and Bertram. Parolles has been exposed as a fool and coward by Helena in Act I, and again by Lafeu in II.v, where he advises Bertram, 'Trust him not in matter of heavy consequence'. Bertram nevertheless keeps him as his confident and counsellor, calling on him in II.iii, 'Go with me to my chamber and advise me'. Clearly Bertram will not or cannot see what others see in Parolles; he knows Parolles as little as he knows Helena, and his judgment of both is super- ficial and fixed in appearances. To him Parolles remains a flamboyant soldier and companion in arms, the friend with whom he can find consolation for his marriage in going to the wars. The focus of the action in the later part of the play is on these two, and on how Bertram may be brought to see more clearly, and to accept Helena as his wife in deed, not just in name.

The central episode in this part of the play is the unmasking of Parolles in IV.iii, and the opening of Bertram's eyes to the fact that his 'devoted friend' and constant companion is no more than a 'Damnable both-sides rogue'. As one who lives by words, by the reputation he makes for himself in talk, Parolles cannot resist undertaking to recapture from the enemy the drum captured by them, though he knows the task to be well-nigh impossible. In the splendidly funny sequence in which he is caught and blindfolded by soldiers of his own side, but deceived by their mumbo-jumbo into thinking he is in the hands of the enemy, he shows himself ready to say anything to save his life. He freely slanders the captains of the French army, including his patron, Bertram; indeed, he utters such gross lies that if he were really in enemy hands, what he says would be of no use to them. This is fine entertainment for all, but it emerges from the letter found on Parolles that he is trying to supplant Bertram in the favours of Diana, and that his lying, cheating and deceiving extend to the betrayal of the most intimate interests of the Count.

At last the blindfold is removed, and Parolles is left, as the soldiers suppose, to his shame; but not a bit of it:

> Yet am I thankful. If my heart were great,
> 'Twould burst at this. Captain I'll be no more,
> But I will eat, and drink, and sleep as soft
> As captain shall. Simply the thing I am
> Shall make me live.
>
> (IV.iii.307)

Exposed as a braggart, he will simply change roles, secure in the expectation that he will live as soft as any captain. Nothing can knock Parolles down for long. His lies, his boasting, his very clothes, as he struts about through the court and battlefield covered in scarves and banners, the most military man of all, are so gross and outrageous as not seriously to take people in, or not for long. He recovers rapidly from disaster, as was shown earlier when Lafeu beat him in II.iii, and his vitality and his outrageousness are signs of a richness of imagination and fertility of invention that are entertaining in themselves. Parolles emerges as more than simply a damnable rogue; he is also an engaging comic figure, whose nastiness is masked and made amusing by his inventiveness and sheer power of survival.

Yet why should Bertram of all others trust him and make of him a bosom friend? One reason sometimes offered is his youth; Bertram apparently is very young when he is sent off to court as an 'unseasoned courtier' and ward of the King in the opening scene, and Parolles has the flashiness and plausibility, as well as a boasted store of experience, to attract him. In addition, the vitality of Parolles is in itself fascinating. Helena, who sees through him from the start, yet sports and talks with him; and Lafeu, who is equally clearsighted about him, and tells him he is 'a general offence, and every man should beat thee' (II.iii.247), yet takes him into his service at the end of the play: 'though you are a fool and a knave, you shall eat'. The Countess's view of Parolles as 'a very tainted fellow, and full of wickedness' (III.ii.85), and as a corrupter of Bertram, is only a partial truth. The taint and wickedness lie in all, potentially at any rate. Lafeu says of him:

> I think thou wast created for men to breathe themselves
> upon thee.
>
> (II.iii.249)

He means by 'breathe', 'exercise their weapons', but his words might be taken in a less literal sense to indicate another aspect of Parolles, the extent to which he acts as a scapegoat who can carry away and neutralize the faults and fears of others. Bertram's attachment to him has been accounted for in this way, that he in the large sense 'breathes himself' on Parolles, who embodies his faults; the unmasking and shaming of Parolles in IV.iii may then be seen as a kind of purifying of the Count.

None of these explanations accounts for Bertram's trust in Parolles, or for his behaviour at the end of the play. For when Bertram is at last forced to confront his own actions in the final scene of the play, he shows that he can lie as well as Parolles. At first, thinking Helena to be dead, he says he loves her; then he lies about the ring he thinks he gave Diana, and though the King, his mother and Lafeu all swear they saw Helena wearing it, still he sullenly persists in saying, 'She never saw it', hopefully thinking they can prove nothing. Again, when faced with Diana, he accuses her falsely of being a prostitute in an attempt to discredit her testimony. It is only when he can wriggle free no more from the weight of evidence against him that he finally confesses what he tried to do, and acknowledges Helena as his wife in more than name. Parolles had asked, 'Who cannot be crush'd with a plot?' (IV.iii.302), when he was exposed, and now it is the turn of Bertram to be crushed as he tries, like Parolles, to dodge his responsibilities, and finds that in the end they cannot be evaded.

If Bertram has something of Parolles in him, then the question why Helena should pursue him with such determination seems even more difficult to answer. His youth pleads for him, and his beauty, if we may trust Helena's starry-eyed image of him as god-like; also the revelation at the end of his lies and shifts as he is forced back upon the truth may appear to some extent as a testing of him, or even an expulsion of what is bad in him. All this is not, however, enough to account for him or for Helena's devotion to him. Indeed, she does not seek to know what he is as a man, but is content with what she imagines him to be; and she never troubles to discover whether Bertram cares for her. In her own way she is as self-centred as Bertram and Parolles, as she starts off resolved to have one man, willy-nilly: 'my intents are fix'd, and will not leave me' (I.i.215). She differs from them in being presented sympathetically from the beginning, praised by most, and acquiring a special grace in the cure of the King. Dramatically the gap between what she is (wise, virtuous, fair – we have the King's word for this), and what she does in making Bertram the object of her devotion and pursuit (the shifty, callow and opinionated Bertram, as he shows himself to be) is not explained, nor is it explicable. The peculiar effect of the play lies in this kind of gap. There is little to suggest that Bertram, or anyone except Parolles, has learned by experience, and as if one near-disaster in arranged marriages were not enough, the play ends with the King of France about to haul out again his parcel of noble bachelors, this time to offer Diana a husband:

Choose thou thy husband, and I'll pay thy dower.

Perhaps another bachelor will not unreasonably cry, like Bertram:

In such a business give me leave to use
The help of mine own eyes.

These discordances give the play its peculiar edge. Where Orlando and Rosalind, and Benedick and Beatrice seem fitly matched, and choose each other for themselves, kept something short of ideal only as a play of mockery about them reveals their humanity and frailty, here in the later comedy, *All's Well that Ends Well*, Helena pursues Bertram without troubling to know what he is like, or whether he wants her, and he is forced to marry her because of a King's power to arrange marriages. Instead of sweetness, there is a jarring note, as if those elements that remain subsidiary in the earlier comedies, like Touchstone's dubious marriage to Audrey, or Claudio's harsh repudiation of Hero in church, take over and partially disrupt the world of high romance. In the effort to understand what Shakespeare was doing, critics have been tempted to find here a religious play in which Helena is a 'channel or medium for the divine or cosmic powers', or an attempt to write a moral play on the problem, where do true honour and nobility lie?[1] An account of the play that focuses on the dramatic action suggests a different estimate of *All's Well*, as something other than festive comedy, it is true, but a modified version of it. Bertram's inadequacies, and Helena's obsession with him, return us, like other inexplicables in the play, to the intractable nature of things as they are. This imposes itself on what might have been a straightforward romantic comedy primarily through an action in which the irrepressible Parolles, and the sardonic clown Lavache, set the tone. Indeed, Lavache has little other function in the play than this. In IV.v, Lafeu tells the Clown that he is, like Parolles, 'both knave and fool', and Lavache admits to being of the devil's party. Yet in some curious way he is, like Parolles, indispensable. As Helena and then Bertram need Parolles to talk with, so the Countess and Lafeu rely on Lavache; though agreeing that he is 'a shrewd knave and unhappy', Lafeu goes on to say, 'I like him well'. Parolles and Lavache seem to represent something in the bedrock of human beings; something of what they are is present in all, as, for example, the lust of the flesh that drives Lavache to think of marriage in I.iii, also urges Bertram to the bed of Diana later on, and perhaps has analogies with that lust of the eye which drives Helena to seek Bertram. The world of romance, the story of deserving but poor beauty marrying a handsome prince, is never free in this play from the vision of things as seen by Parolles and Lavache, with earthy realism: 'If men could be contented to be what they are, there were no fear in marriage' (I.iii.51).

(ii) *Measure for Measure*

In *Measure for Measure* too a striking feature of the play almost from the beginning is the powerful presence of a clown, Pompey, and a corrupting lover of words, like Parolles, in the

[1] See G. Wilson Knight, 'The Third Eye', in K, Muir, *Shakespeare; The Comedies*, p. 151; and M. C. Bradbrook, 'Virtue is the True Nobility', *Review of English Studies*, XXVI (1950), 288-301, also reprinted in Muir, pp. 119-32. G. K. Hunter, in his Introduction to the New Arden edition (1959), pp. xix, lviii, remarks on the play's 'sombre tone', and on its 'attempt to express complex thought'; what seems rather to emerge strongly in production is its lightness of tone, and its lack of concern, as a dramatic action, with problems as such.

figure of Lucio. They enter in the second scene, where Mistress
Overdone is introduced also; their liveliness, good humour, and
freedom are important in establishing the tonality of the play.
News of the plucking down of all brothels disturbs Mistress
Overdone and her bawd Pompey only for a moment:

> *Mis. O.*   Why, here's a change indeed in the commonwealth!
> What shall become of me?
> *Pompey*   Come, fear not you: good counsellors lack no clients.
> Though you change your place, you need not change
> trade: I'll be your tapster still. Courage, there will be
> pity taken on you; you that have worn your eyes
> almost out in the service, you will be considered.
>
> (I.ii.98)

The stance here recalls Parolles', 'simply the thing I am shall
make me live'; what is primary in the presentation of these
characters is not their nature as sinners, or their licentiousness,
but simply their vitality, their zest for life. The action of the
first part of the play, as it involves Angelo, Claudio and Isabella,
develops in relation to Pompey's exuberant existence and defiance of repression, and against a world of bawdy talk and of
bawdy houses where there is no lack of clients.

Measured against this, the actions of Angelo and Isabella
appear harsh, extreme, even absurd. Claudio, contracted to
Juliet, is sentenced to death for lack only of what he calls 'the
denunciation . . . of outward order' (I.ii.141); they are married,
in other words, according to English common law, though the
religious ceremony and public announcement are lacking. For
Claudio to be sentenced to prison on this account, while bawds
walk free, is outrageous; for him to be sentenced to death is
nothing short of monstrous. As Claudio is marched off un-
willingly to prison, so his sister Isabella is seen complaining that
the rules of the votarists of St Clare are not strict enough;
chastity, poverty, obedience, silence and virtual imprisonment
are something less than she desires, 'wishing a more strict
restraint Upon the sisterhood' (I.iv.4). The juxtaposition of,
on the one hand, freedom, common vitality, licence and lechery,
against, on the other hand, Angelo's urge to impose extreme
penalties, and Isabella's drive to inflict on herself the maximum
discipline and restraint, provide the tonality of the play.

These ironic contrasts are developed further in Act II, which opens with the long scene of the trial of Pompey. It seems that when Claudio was arrested, he did not try to defend himself, but admitted the offence, to the extent of having had too much liberty in getting Juliet with child; at any rate we do not see him tried, but he enters already sentenced, and on his way to prison. In II.i, however, Angelo and Escalus sit in full state as judges to determine the case of those two 'notorious benefactors', Pompey the bawd and Froth a foolish gentleman. Elbow the Constable has too much of Dogberry about him to present his case with any clarity, and Pompey has no great difficulty in turning the evidence, filibustering, and introducing so much irrelevance that all sense gets lost, He wearies Angelo into withdrawing, and although Escalus, hearing it out, recognizes that Pompey, who calls himself a tapster, has been practising as a bawd, he can do nothing at the end but send him off with a warning. It is again a lively and very funny scene; Pompey's meandering tale of Mistress Elbow's longing for prunes, like the rest of his patter in the scene, is made doubly funny by the continual innuendo which Elbow and Froth fail to understand. Pompey manages to suggest that Froth, Elbow and Elbow's wife all have some connection with the stews. It appears that Pompey has provided Froth with a mistress in Elbow's wife, who has been pretty free in her favours anyway; as Pompey says, 'There was nothing done to her once'. If they have offended, then, in making a whore of Elbow's wife, Pompey and Froth have committed a much worse crime than Claudio and Juliet; but the whole thing is a tangle, and is presented so comically that even Escalus as judge can only join in the fun:

Elbow	Prove this, thou wicked Hannibal, or I'll have mine action of battery on thee.
Escalus	If he took you a box on th'ear, you might have your action of slander too.
Elbow	Marry, I thank your good worship for it. What is't your worship's pleasure I shall do with this wicked caitiff?
Escalus	Truly, officer, because he hath some offences in him which thou wouldst discover if thou couldst, let him continue in his courses till thou know'st what they are.

(II.i.169)

This comic perspective on the demands of the flesh is followed at once by the meeting of Isabella, come to plead for Claudio's life, and Angelo. As in the scene in *All's Well* in which Helena cures the King, Shakespeare changes the key, so to speak, endowing the earnestness of Angelo and Isabella with a religious colouring. Isabella appeals to Christ in her plea for mercy:

> Why, all the souls that were were forfeit once,
> And He that might the vantage best have took
> Found out the remedy.

> (II.ii.73)

As their interchanges develop through the second act, Angelo sees himself becoming a devil, and the overtones of his name seem to allude to the fall of Lucifer. Locally this is powerful, and Angelo's self-amazement and temporary disgust at the discovery of his lust are strongly realized.[1] The whole sequence, however, is tempered by what has gone before. If Pompey's licence in sexual matters needs to be restrained, at least his instinct as 'a poor fellow that would live' seems healthier than Angelo's and Isabella's shrinking from the demands of the flesh. Angelo indeed, tormented by Isabella's beauty, comes in these scenes to admit that his blood, far from being 'snow-broth' as Lucio had said, is as hot as other men's; 'Blood, thou art blood', he cries in pained acknowledgment of what in the arrogance of conscious virtue he had denied. So Isabella's chastity is rather a repudiation of the flesh than an acceptance of Christ.

It is striking that in her first interview with Angelo, Lucio stands looking over her shoulder, a kind of Mephistopheles, egging her on not from any interest in virtue, or in the rescue of Claudio, but simply in the enjoyment of the game of winning

[1] Those who dwell on the themes and moral concerns of the play tend to argue as does F. R. Leavis in a notable essay 'The Greatness of *Measure for Measure*', *Scrutiny*, X (1941-2), 234-47, that 'If we don't see ourselves as Angelo, we have taken the play and the moral very imperfectly' (p. 246). But this is quite to miss the distancing of this character in the action, and the centrality of the Duke, as established by the sequence of the action. Angelo is present in only six scenes on stage, and apart from the two scenes with Isabella in Act II his role is so limited that it is difficult for an actor to sustain it; he speaks only 30 lines, and is present in only one short scene, during the whole of the thousand or so lines of Acts III and IV.

Angelo over, through the exercise of rhetoric and the warmth of her personality. He is a strange companion for the 'saintly' Isabella. It is true that the scenes in which Angelo confronts Isabella with his demand that she sleep with him to save her brother, and the scene in which Claudio begs Isabella to save his life at the cost of her virginity, are written with a poetic intensity, and here the inflexibilities of character come into serious collision with the inflexibilities of the law. Nevertheless, it is important to distinguish between the way the characters see themselves, and the pattern of expectations set up from the start of the action, with its promise of a comic resolution. Angelo's inflexible addiction to the letter of the law in the case of Claudio is followed by his equally outrageous demand that Isabella commit with him the very offence for which he has sentenced Claudio to death. Isabella's absolute valuation of her chastity above life:

> Isabel, live chaste, and brother die:
> More than our brother is our chastity.

(II.iv.184)

is followed by her terrible and total rejection of Claudius when he begs her to save him:

> Take my defiance,
> Die; perish! might but my bending down
> Reprieve thee from thy fate, it should proceed.
> I'll pray a thousand prayers for thy death,
> No word to save thee.

(III.i.144)

Angelo and Isabella are off balance, lacking a sense of proportion, or a sense of humour, as is brought out by the contrast between them and Pompey and Mistress Overdone.

Their inflexible stances are further set off against the bearing of the Duke, who has already appeared in his disguise as a Friar in I.iii, where he indicates some suspicion of Angelo. He returns in II.ii to advise Juliet, and again in III.i, to see Claudio and deliver his famous exhortation to him to be 'absolute for death'. Claudio is for a time persuaded by his reasoning that life is not worth having, as subject to afflictions and diseases, unhappy, and nursed by baseness; as compounded out of dust,

and limited by the transitoriness of this world where death may
strike at any moment:

> Thou hast nor youth nor age,
> But as it were an after-dinner's sleep,
> Dreaming on both; for all thy blessed youth
> Becomes as aged, and doth beg the alms
> Of palsied eld: and when thou art old and rich,
> Thou hast neither heat, affection, limb, nor beauty
> To make thy riches pleasant. What's yet in this
> That bears the name of life?

(III.i.32)

The Duke's rhetoric is splendid, and the speech justly celebrated, for it strikes plangently a chord to which all human
beings respond, and which echoes Christian homilies on the
vanity of this world, and on the art of dying well. Yet his account
of the human condition 'eliminates its spiritual aspect, and is
essentially materialist and pagan';[1] if life were really like this,
then suicide would be the natural way out. What this 'Friar'
advises corresponds closely enough with the counsel of Despair
in Spenser's *Faerie Queene*, who spells out the implications:

> Then doe no further goe, no further stray,
> But here lie downe, and to thy rest betake
> Th'ill to prevent that life ensewen may.
> For what hath life, that may it loved make,
> And gives not rather cause it to forsake?
> Feare, sicknesse, age, losse, labour, sorrow, strife;
> Paine, hunger, cold, that makes the hart to quake;
> And ever fickle fortune rageth rife,
> All which, and thousands mo do make a loathsome life.

(I.ix.44)

If life corresponds to the Duke's description of it here, there
would be little point in Angelo and Isabella taking their per-
emptory and rigid attitudes; Angelo's lust to possess Isabella,
and her concern for chastity, have become more important to
them than life or death. These drives in them, together with
Angelo's anxiety to preserve his 'unsoil'd name', are what make
their lives important to them, and yet paradoxically make
them careless of life in others. The attitudes they take would

---

[1] J. W. Lever, Introduction to the New Arden edition of *Measure for Measure*
(1965), p. lxxxvii, where there is a fine analysis of the implications of this speech.

result in the death of Claudio, and both are destructive of life. Claudio's initial acceptance of the Duke's counsel, 'To sue to live, I find I seek to die' (III.i.42) is a contradiction of that natural urge that brought him and Juliet together to create new life, an urge echoed with a poignant irony in his cry:

> If I must die,
> I will encounter darkness as a bride
> And hug it in mine arms.

(III.i.84)

His repudiation of this acceptance of death, and cry to Isabella to save him, are not in this context the appeals of a coward, but cries from the heart of one who loves life, whose life is love, a love that contrasts in its warmth with the chill austerity of Angelo and the frigid chastity of Isabella. Shakespeare, however, does not let him get away with it and command our sympathy thus easily. Claudio does not mention Juliet in his pleading with Isabella, but thinks only of himself; what's more, his appeal to her, 'Ay, but to die, and go we know not where . . .' (III.i.119), springs not from a love of life, but from a horror of death and dread of what comes after. To be absolute for life in this way is as perverse as to be absolute for death in the Duke's way.

The inadequacies of the Duke's homily, and of Claudio's plea for his life, help to maintain an uneasy balance of sympathies in the scene, and Isabella's final shrill denunciation of Claudio seems almost warranted. For a moment it appears that no solution is possible, and the harsh polarities established in the action and in the speeches in this scene reflect in their bleakest extremity the oppositions which form the basis of the dramatic shaping of the play. In fact, the return of the Duke in disguise to watch over Angelo's rule in Vienna is itself sufficient indication that all will be set to rights in the end; and at the very point when a resolution of conflict seems impossible, the Duke appears again, immediately after Claudio's interview with Isabella, dropping into prose and effecting another change of key to restore something of an earlier tone and mood. He produces the solution in Mariana of the moated grange, married to Angelo as truly as Juliet is married to Claudio, by civil contract, and a happy outcome is assured. This confirms the drift of the action from the opening scenes, which is on the side

of life, not death. The development of the conflicts between
Angelo and Isabella, and between Isabella and Claudio, to the
crisis of III.i shows horrifyingly the limitations of being absolute
for death in the way Isabella and Angelo are, and displays also
the inadequacies of being absolute for life in the way Claudio
and, by implication, Pompey and his fellows are. So now we
see Pompey and Mistress Overdone conveyed to prison as
bawd and prostitute, and the prison, emblem of the law's
restraint upon the lusts of men, remains the centre of the play's
action almost until the final unravelling in Act V. The prison is
curiously also a centre of life. Pompey exchanges the role of
cheerful bawd for that of equally cheerful hangman. Lucio
appears there, refusing to bail Pompey, and slandering the
disguised Duke; he too, it seems, may be condemned for
lechery, and has, like Angelo and Claudio, promised marriage:
'Mistress Kate Keep-down was with child by him in the Duke's
time, he promised her marriage' (III.ii.187). It seems that on all
sides the demands of the flesh, or the natural drive of life,
asserts itself, as Pompey had said earlier to Escalus:

> *Escalus* But the law will not allow it, Pompey, nor it shall not
> be allowed in Vienna.
> *Pompey* Does your worship mean to geld and splay all the
> youth of the city?
> *Escalus* No, Pompey.
> *Pompey* Truly, sir, in my poor opinion, they will to't then.
>
> (II.i.216)

Even the Duke carries some smack of mere humanity in his
long interchange with Lucio; it is not that he is, as Lucio says,
a lecher who would 'mouth with a beggar, though she smelt
brown bread and garlic' (III.ii.170), but that he is a man of
flesh, subject to common lusts and desires. There is no need to
speculate whether Lucio penetrates the Duke's disguise here;
the point is that by hobnobbing with all and sundry, the Duke
becomes what Lucio calls him, a 'fantastical Duke of dark
corners' (IV.iii.151), rather enjoying his intrigues and man-
œuvres. The Duke deceives and lies, deceives Claudio and
Escalus by concealing his plot from them, usurping a beggary
he was never born to, as Lucio says, and the tricks that go with
it. The dialogue puts him and Lucio on an equal footing for a

time, as Lucio nudges him, and takes him by the elbow in confidential gossip. This is why Act III has to end with the Duke's choric speech in rhymed couplets:

> He who the sword of Heaven will bear
> Should be as holy as severe . . . .

(III.ii.243)

This is designed to restore his authority as ruler and justice, and comes as a reminder of the undisguised Duke in the middle of his performance in another role, that of intriguing Friar.

Some have seen the Duke as a heavenly figure, or as an image of James I, from whose book of advice to his son, *Basilikon Doron*, some of his precepts are garnered.[1] The King may have been pleased to find some reflection of himself at the court performance in December 1604, and perhaps did not notice that the Duke has brought about the present state of affairs in Vienna, and that besides deceiving others, he is deceived himself, as now Angelo, having, as he thinks, possessed Isabella, fails to keep the promise he made, and sends an order for the execution instead of the pardon of Claudio. In Act IV the Duke is really put to his shifts to save him, and is only enabled to do so in the end by a mere accident – the death of the unseen pirate Ragozine from fever, whose head can conveniently stand in for that of Claudio. For at this point the Duke encounters another force for life in prison, in the person of Barnardine, a prisoner of nine years' standing, who, though sentenced to death, has managed to remain alive by simply refusing to die at anyone's convenience. Although he would be an appropriate stand-in for the doomed Claudio, and an obvious candidate to provide a substitute head to be sent to Angelo, he is never in a fit state to be executed, and obstinately lives on. As the Provost describes him, he is:

---

[1] Recent studies which emphasize a Christian reading of the play include Nevill Coghill's 'Comic Form in *Measure for Measure*', *Shakespeare Survey*, 8 (1955), 14-27, and Raymond Southall's '*Measure for Measure* and the Protestant Ethic', *Essays in Criticism*, X (1961), 10-33. The latter sees the play as an 'ideological battle over the concept of Grace'. On the possible connections of the Duke with King James, see especially Josephine Waters Bennett, '*Measure for Measure*' *as Royal Entertainment* (1966) and David Lloyd Stevenson, 'The Historical Dimension in *Measure for Measure*: The Role of James I in the Play', *ELH*, XXVI (1959), 188-208. The latter is reprinted as an Appendix in his *The Achievement of 'Measure for Measure'* (1966).

A man that apprehends death no more dreadfully but as a
drunken sleep; careless, reckless, and fearless of what's past,
present, or to come; insensible of mortality, and desperately
mortal.

(IV.ii.134)

In the Provost's view, Barnardine lacks any sensibility with
regard to death, and appears 'desperately mortal', in a desperate
condition, as doomed to die, and perhaps as without hope of
grace. However, the one thing that is clear from Barnardine's
behaviour is that by declining to receive advice, and refusing
to prepare himself for death, he keeps himself alive, rendering
the Duke unable to have the sentence carried out: 'to transport
him in the mind he is Were damnable' (IV.iii.64).

Barnardine embodies a defiance and rejection of the Duke's
exhortation to Claudio, and a denial of that account of life:

> Thy best of rest is sleep,
> And that thou oft provok'st; yet grossly fear'st
> Thy death, which is no more.

(III.i.17)

Barnardine fears death no more than a drunken sleep, yet will
not be executed, and indeed survives to be pardoned at the end
of the play. His obstinacy precipitates the Duke's decision to
reveal himself, and call Angelo and Escalus to meet him at the
city gates. Again, it is the urge to live, not the resolution for
death, that carries through the play's action. Now Angelo, his
intended crime revealed, is so smitten by guilt as to demand
his own death, and the Duke, in response, puts on an authority
like that shown earlier by Angelo, crying:

> An Angelo for Claudio, death for death!
> Haste still pays haste, and leisure answers leisure,
> Like doth quit like, and Measure still for Measure.

(V.i.407)

It takes this demand of an eye for an eye, the full rigour of the
law, to soften Isabella, who joins Mariana to beg for Angelo's
life; and this softening in her, this yielding from her puritanical
fastidiousness to beg mercy for a man of acknowledged sin,
seems to prepare the way for the Duke to propose marriage
with her. Claudio and Juliet are restored to freedom and to one
another; and Lucio, his gross calumnies of the Duke as 'a

fleshmonger, a fool, and a coward' exposed, finds that his words recoil upon himself, as he is forced to marry the woman he wronged.

The last act unravels all with its series of confrontations and revelations, enabling the play's title to exert a quibbling meaning in several ways; the obvious significance, of punishment to fit the crime, relates to Angelo chiefly, though, more liberally interpreted, it fits the case of Lucio at the end; the phrase also suggests plot countering plot, as the Duke's measures work against those of Angelo; and also dance or movement for movement, implying a balance in plot and rhythm, a balance worked out in the comic resolution of pardon and marriage. Of that world of bawdy vitality so prominent in the earlier part of the play, only two representatives, Lucio and Barnardine, are seen in the last act, and the latter has no speaking part. They are not necessary here because the momentum of the action is clear, but the sprightly Lucio is given some rein to mock at others, and slander freely with imputations of lechery, until in unmasking the Friar to find the Duke, he finds he has unmasked himself for what he is. Lucio's lechery is as harmful and unbalanced as the prim rigour of Angelo and Isabella, and the balance and harmony symbolized by marriage terminate the action for him as for Angelo and Isabella – and for all three marriage may have the nature of a recovery of health, a punishment, and an expiation, or a full acceptance of the natural inclinations and responsibilities of a human being. The play leaves us to determine in just what 'measure' any of these applies.

There is a good deal of commentary on *All's Well* and *Measure for Measure* which presents them, and certainly with some justice, as verging on allegory, or at any rate as plays of ideas. Titles like '*Measure for Measure* and the Gospels', or '*Measure for Measure* and the Christian Doctrine of Atonement' suggest the degree to which the religious elements may be stressed.[1]

[1] The first is from G. Wilson Knight's chapter on the play in *The Wheel of Fire* (1930), the second from the essay by R. W. Battenhouse in *P.M.L.A.*, LXI (1946), 1029-59.

C

When Helena persuades the King in *All's Well* to submit to her cure of his disease, the rhymed verse of that scene conveys a sense almost of ritual, and the language is inspirational, with its echoes of the Bible, and invocations of God and Heaven. Again, in *Measure for Measure* the cluster of scenes at the end of Act II and beginning of Act III emphasize with a religious intensity the crisis of conscience in Angelo and in Isabella. Angelo, self-consciously become devilish in lust, is sharply aware of his sin; Isabella, a novice in the order of Poor Clares, makes her virginity the test of a Christian life; and the Duke in his role of Friar brings spiritual advice to Claudio in prison, carrying the emphasis through more strongly in this play, as he emerges from his disguise at the end of Act III to moralize on the function of the good ruler, and again in Act V, for Angelo to see in him the agent of Heaven:

> I should be guiltier than my guiltiness
> To think I can be undiscernible
> When I perceive your Grace, like power divine,
> Hath look'd upon my passes.

(V.i.365)

These elements in the plays are important, but it is a distortion of their total effect to dwell on them alone, and see, for example, in *Measure for Measure* a 'treatment of the themes of Justice and Mercy, Grace and Nature, Creation and Death'.[1] For then it will appear that Shakespeare's 'creative energy is deeply engaged'[2] only in the clash of absolutes in the confrontation of Angelo and Isabella, and Isabella and Claudio, that is to say in scenes of poetic intensity and tragic possibilities. It seems to me that Shakespeare's creative energy is just as deeply engaged in the writing of the scenes involving Parolles, Lucio, Pompey Bum and Barnardine, who are not simply, as is sometimes suggested, 'men of sin'. Something more complicated is happening in these plays. It has been well said in a recent essay on *Measure for Measure* that in this play

> a wholly satisfying evaluation of human actions goes beyond
> our ability to classify them according to categories of virtue
> fixed by theologians or by statutory law. Whether such actions

[1] J. W. Lever in the New Arden edition, p. lxiii.
[2] *Ibid.*, p. lxix.

be technically good or evil, technically legal or illegal, we are made aware that we truly evaluate them by the less conditioned, more nearly morally intuitive responses of that side of us which operates below the level of conscious dogma.

Below the neat 'surface design of evil committed and evil caught out', the play suggests deeper evaluations of the attitudes and conduct of the characters, evaluations which do not 'conform to the warm, well-lighted world of institutionalized good and evil we all wish to think we inhabit'.[1] These deeper evaluations are brought home by the totality of the play, and arise from the interplay between the surface design as it involves Helena and the King, or Isabella and Angelo, and the deeper complexities of the dramatic action as a whole. What proves dominant in *All's Well* is something like Bernard Shaw's life force, as exemplified in Ann Whitefield in *Man and Superman*, pursuing the reluctant Jack Tanner across half of Europe into marriage; so the urge to lose her virginity to Bertram drives Helena, and his mere vitality enables Parolles to retain some sort of place about the court against all odds. In *Measure for Measure* too, where the restraint upon Claudio's 'too much liberty', and upon Pompey's and Lucio's too much lechery, are in part justified, nevertheless liberty and love, energy for life and acceptance of the desires of the flesh control the movement of the action.

In this larger perspective, the 'miracle-working' of Helena, who becomes for a brief time, and incidentally, heaven's agent in curing the King, appears also as a device to elevate a girl of low birth and to establish fully her moral superiority to Bertram, her moral worth counterpoising his nobility of rank. The absoluteness of Isabella and Angelo, however strong their sense of moral urgency, their self-questioning, their confusion of sin and guilt, law and mercy, chastity and honour, comes over as life-defeating and destructive, in relation to the larger movement of the play. Both plays raise serious 'issues', and can be described in terms of 'themes' and 'ideas', but the explorations – for example of the nuances of 'virtue' as opposed to 'honour' in *All's Well*, or of the more fundamental clashes of incompatibles in *Measure for Measure* – are bound in by the action as a whole, and subdued by the intractable nature of life at large, by the inexplicable sense of a desire for survival, and by excitement in

---

[1] David Lloyd Stevenson, *The Achievement of 'Measure for Measure'*, p. 61.

living, that breezy pleasure exhibited in the lovemakers, lechers, fools and clowns, in Parolles, in Lucio, in Pompey, and in Barnardine, who will not die. The anguish of Angelo is powerful as he yields to his lust for Isabella, and it is rendered through his deep sense of the moral issues involved:

> O cunning enemy, that, to catch a saint,
> With saints dost bait thy hook! Most dangerous
> Is that temptation that doth goad us on
> To sin in loving virtue.

(II.ii.180)

At the same time, in the perspective of the dramatic action as a whole, this scene is one of the means by which his shrill and harsh rigidity and self-righteousness are repudiated; so it is also with Isabella, as both are brought to accept love, mercy and marriage at the end.

Like *All's Well*, *Measure for Measure* is in the end an uncomfortable play because in spite of the marriages that round it off, it forces on us a sense of the gap between belief and act, between what people would be and what they are, or between justice and charity. So, for instance, there is no way of accounting judicially or ethically for the stubborn Barnardine; it is not clear whether the marriage of Angelo to Mariana is more a reward or a punishment to both of them; the Duke's impending marriage to Isabella goes unexplained; and all through virtue gains no notable victories in opposition to licentiousness, but rather loses out in its strictness, while licentiousness carries in it a love of life that wins sympathy and seems generous by contrast. If 'liberty plucks justice by the nose' (I.iii.29), this tends to prove beneficial in curbing the harshness of the law, and shows how there can indeed be 'a charity in sin' (II.iv.63), as Angelo and Isabella agree there may, but without seeing the implications of what they are saying. The last act is neat in its contrivance of measure for measure, but the dramatic effect of the play stems from the gap between that neatness and what remains unexplained and unresolved below the surface. Some see mere confusion in this, and not an effect sought by Shakespeare; and some regard the play as limited in its achievement because 'the "incarnation" of ideas, principles, beliefs is not at all points consistent and complete'.[1] A study of the dramatic

---

[1] J. W. Lever in the New Arden edition, p. xciii.

shaping of the play suggests rather that such a reading is made too plausible by some aspects of what is not basically a drama attempting such consistency. In other words, the weakness of *Measure for Measure* lies not in its failure to maintain the 'incarnation' of beliefs found in Act II and the beginning of Act III, but rather in the overweighting of these scenes. The strong religious feeling here seems to invite too close an involvement with some characters in an action which is generally more concerned with a critical placing of them. The change of key in Act III seems too marked and too abrupt, the revelation of Mariana too easy a way out, and the Duke has too much responsibility as a character here in holding the action together. If Shakespeare had given a serious weight to the action in wholly secular terms, he might have been able to control the play's balance more easily.

(iii) JONSON, MARSTON AND SATIRE

Troilus and Cressida differs from the other dark comedies in its pagan setting, and in this play Shakespeare was able to establish the background of values in secular terms. It may seem odd to come to this play as the last for discussion, since its possible connection with the war of the poets, and the stationers' register entry for it in February 1603, would suggest that it may have been the first of the three to be written. However this may be, it has claims to be regarded as the finest achievement among them. What seems clear is that they form a group, that they were all written at some time in the years 1601-4, and that they have some connection with the general change of direction in the development of the drama at this period. In particular, they can be related to the new vogue for satirical plays at this time. It is important, however, to try to determine just what these links were, and not to jump too readily to the conclusion that Shakespeare took over a convention of 'comical satire' as established by Ben Jonson.[1]

---

[1] As O. J. Campbell argued rather crudely in *Comicall Satyre and Shakespeare's 'Troilus and Cressida'* (1938). In this book, and in *Shakespeare's Satire* (1943), the critical argument is presented tendentiously and without much sensitivity, but both books are important because their author was among the first to relate Shakespeare's problem comedies to the growth of satire in the period.

Jonson's experiments in writing plays he called 'comical satires' began with *Every Man out of his Humour*, acted by Shakespeare's company probably late in 1599, and printed in 1600; it was the first of his plays to be published. The Induction and Commentary by Cordatus and Mitis in this make clear how conscious Jonson was of classical precedent and example in the writing of comedy and of satire. The opening speech of Asper recalls Juvenal on the impossibility of not writing satire in an age of vice and folly, but echoes also Marston and the other satirists of the 1590s who also cried out in Asper's vein:

> my language
> Was never ground into such oily colours,
> To flatter vice, and daub iniquity:
> But (with an armed and resolved hand)
> I'll strip the ragged follies of the time
> Naked as at their birth —
>
> (Induction, l. 13)

Formal verse satire based on Latin models, primarily Juvenal, was a new development in English poetry in the late sixteenth century. The poets seem to have been confused about the origin and nature of what they were doing, understandably enough, since they inherited a confused tradition. The word 'satire' was thought to relate both to Latin 'satura', a medley, and to the Greek 'satyr', suggesting the rough manner adopted by, for instance, Marston and Donne, who supposed that the proper style for satire should be 'characteristically harsh and obscure'.[1]

This confusion may be seen as reflecting a more radical artistic problem. The harsh voice of the satirist lashed out at his age:

> O Age of rusty iron! Some better wit
> Call it some worse name, if ought equal it;
>
> (Donne, Satire V, l. 35)

This note of hatred and invective showed the honesty and passion of the speaker, but also led him in his medley of a poem into such involvement with the characters and scenes he vividly depicted in order to demonstrate their reality and power, that he might seem to be contaminated by them. Donne plays wittily

---

[1] Citing Antony Caputi, *John Marston, Satirist* (1961), p. 25.

upon this in his Satire IV, in which he goes to Court, having 'no suit there, nor new suit to show', but out of mere curiosity and pride, to condemn all he finds there:

> hast thou seen,
> O Sun, in all thy journey, Vanity,
> Such as swells the bladder of our court?

(l. 166)

The attack on vanity is here strengthened by the poet's opening admission that he has sinned himself in going to court in order to describe what he saw there: 'My sin indeed is great' (l. 1). In this poem, the speaker retires into 'wholesome solitariness' after his visit to court, in order to launch his general onslaught against 'Vanity'.

Donne's manœuvre here shows his awareness of a difficulty. The satirist offered an attack on some vice or folly, usually a single vice in each satire, in order to recommend a corresponding virtue. In doing this he was likely to be forced into contradictory stances; he had to show intimate knowledge of the vice, and so seem perhaps to be himself touched by it, and yet retain a lofty remoteness from it in order to condemn it; his horror at vice might point in the direction of withdrawal into 'wholesome solitariness' to allow him full scope for denunciation, but this would seem to draw him towards the position of misanthrope; his necessary intimacy with it might on the other hand suggest an enjoyment of it, and draw him into the stance of the ale-house wit, engaged and basically satisfied with the society he castigates. The satirist might take one of several stances within these extremes; one position is that of the man of independent good sense, seeing the truth more clearly than others, as in Donne's Satire III; another is that of the cynic, seeing nothing but 'foul filth' in humanity, as in Marston's Satire VII in *The Scourge of Villainy*; a third is that of melancholy malcontent, as in Marston's Satire IX, where he 'vomits forth' his hate; and a fourth is that of humorist, gently mocking but rather enjoying the folly he sees, and singing 'in sporting merriment', as in Marston's Satire X. At one extreme the satirist appears as a malcontent, a melancholy man, savagely denouncing the sins of the world, and at the other extreme as a genial comedian, tolerantly amused by follies he enjoys.

Another problem for the satirist was noted by Marston in his final word in *The Scourge of Villainy*, his note to the reader, expressing his fear of being misinterpreted by those who, 'being ignorant, not knowing the nature of a Satire (which is under fained private names, to note general vices), will needs wrest each fained name to a private unfained person'.[1] The variety both of vices and follies attacked 'under fained private names', and of stances taken in different satires by the plain-speaking poet, provided some safeguard against such misinterpretation, but not enough to prevent the anger of the government bursting out in June 1599 with the Archbishop of Canterbury's order banning the publication of satires and epigrams. It seems probable that Ben Jonson was already engaged on the writing of *Every Man out of his Humour* when this order was promulgated, and that formal verse satire had begun to influence the drama. What is clear is that within a short time there arose a new kind of professional children's theatre specializing in plays with a satirical edge to them; the Children of St Paul's were active probably in late 1599, and the Children of the Chapel at Blackfriars by September 1600.

Modern commentators have sought to find an overall shape and argument in Marston's satires, and to resolve the many voices of the satirist into one voice, 'harsh, honest, frank, and filled with indignation', rough, envious, delighting in exposing sins, guilty, sick, and melancholic.[2] This effort to find a unity is a product of hindsight, and a natural desire to establish Marston's quality as a poet. Jonson seems rather to have sensed the variety of voices, and the difficulty of reconciling them. The problems for him of projecting the satirist into drama in his new 'comical satires' were considerable, as *Every Man out of his Humour* illustrates. Asper, the free and independent judge, whose 'strict hand Was made to seize on vice', appears in the Induction, but is kept out of the action; perhaps Jonson realized that such a figure would have had no genuinely dramatic role, but must have appeared as the voice of the author criticizing his own characters. The two satirists in the action are both

---

[1] *The Poems of John Marston*, edited by Arnold Davenport (Liverpool, 1961), p. 176.
[2] These are the 'main features of the satirist's character', as described by Alvin Kernan with reference to Marston in *The Cankered Muse* (New Haven, 1959), p. 116.

interesting and complex figures. Macilente, the poor but honest intellectual, knows how to prize virtue, but, as is made plain early on, envies those more fortunate than himself, so that his criticism of the vice and folly he sees in others is contaminated by his selfishness and malice. At times this becomes pathetic, as in his envy of his friend Deliro for possessing a beautiful wife, Fallace, whom we see to be a silly, vain woman; or later, when Macilente boasts of his superiority to Shift:

> Heart! I do know now, in a fair just cause,
> I dare do more than he, a thousand times;
> Why should they not take knowledge of this, ha!
> And give my worth allowance before his?

> (IV.v.30)

The poor swaggerer Shift is not worth his envy, as Macilente half realizes seeing his 'drunken flourish', but yet he takes a spiteful pleasure in seeing Shift humiliated with the others at the end, 'O, how I do feed upon this now, and fat myself!' (V.iii.75). Macilente's spite is marked by his poisoning of Puntarvolo's dog, a mean act, as Mitis the commentator notes, 'a piece of true envy'. At the end Jonson has Macilente come forward and invite the audience to regard him 'return'd to you as I was Asper at the first', a transformation which may work theatrically in so far as the same actor plays both, but which remains a palpable device.

Carlo Buffone seems designed to oppose Macilente in some ways, a fat character as against a lean one, a buffoon contrasting with a man of envy. Although described in the Induction as 'an impudent common jester' who 'will sooner lose his soul than a jest', Carlo Buffone develops in the play into a much more complicated character. He has something of Macilente's clearsightedness, and both can rail at folly and sin in others; in addition, Carlo Buffone understands Macilente better than Macilente understands himself, as is shown when Carlo leads him to display his satirical zest, and to rail for the benefit of Puntarvolo, commenting aside to the latter, 'How like you him? is't not good spiteful slave? ha? (IV.iv.95). Carlo sees the extent to which Macilente is a 'salt villain' (V.iv.25) for all his pretensions. At the same time, Carlo admires Macilente, joins with him in abusing fools, and in this lacks all scruple, as he admits to Puntarvolo; Macilente at least tries to help and be loyal to his friend Deliro, but Carlo rejects all such concern: 'Pish, the title of a friend, it's a vain idle thing, only venerable among fools' (IV.iii.111). His impudence and inability to resist the temptation to wound with words, lead him to insult Puntarvolo at the end, for which he is punished by having his mouth sealed up with wax. However, Carlo Buffone can also be most engaging, and his good humour makes him in many ways more attractive than Macilente. He provides what is perhaps the funniest sequence in the play when he toasts himself drunk in Act V.

In these two characters Jonson developed in a rich way some of the conflicting impulses in the attitudes embodied in the spokesmen of formal verse satires. Macilente knows what is right, but acts from the wrong motives, envying Sordido, as Cordatus reminds us, 'not as he is a villain, . . . but as he is rich and fortunate' (I.iii.163); Macilente's hatred of vice is self-regarding, and, tarnished by the vices he exposes, and hating good fortune in others, he is in consequence melancholy. Carlo Buffone, who would sacrifice all for a jest, frankly rejects a moral stance, yet enjoys attacking folly and vice, sees through pretensions, and can be warmly engaging as a clown. Asper's stance, that of upright, severe and independent judge, remains simple, like the stance typical of the formal verse satirist confined to one attitude in each satire, only at the cost of total withdrawal from the clashes and mutual criticism within the dramatic action.

Jonson appears to have taken some trouble over preparing the play for publication in 1600, and his consciousness of the experimental nature of what he was doing is shown in the elaborate explanations of humours and of the origins of comedy in the Induction. The commentary of Cordatus amd Mitis, who sit throughout the action watching it, is also designed to answer possible objections and to explain the way satire works in the play. The dramatic action in fact displays an entertaining and engaging group of 'humorous' characters, like Puntarvolo, the romantic knight, and Fastidious Brisk, the would-be courtier, who wastes his estate on clothes; courtier and citizen, student and countryman, are all displayed in their affectations and folly. They are presented with a generous warmth, and much of the play provides good comedy; one weakness indeed emerges in the gap between the bitterness, envy, and professed hostility to vice on Macilente's part, and the relative harmlessness of the genial figures he rails at. The one vicious character, Sordido, is converted to charity and kindness after hearing peasants curse him as they cut him down from the tree on which he has attempted to commit suicide, and remains unaffected by Macilente as the scourger of vice.

The other two plays Jonson described as 'comical satires', *Cynthia's Revels* (printed 1601), and *Poetaster* (printed 1602), were both written for children to act. They are more intellectual and narrower plays than *Every Man out of his Humour*; both plays reflect Jonson's largeness of spirit, and contain characteristically brilliant episodes, but *Cynthia's Revels* restricts itself to court affectations springing from the fountain of self-love, and *Poetaster* most immediately relates to the quarrel of the poets. In Crites of *Cynthia's Revels*, Jonson develops the Asper-figure, 'eager and constant in reproof, without fear controlling the world's abuses', into the critic who combines the best moral and literary standards, and who first ridicules the bad dialogue of the playwright Anaides, and then becomes judge of all the 'self-loving humours' of the courtiers. Crites perhaps too simply embodies the author, and Jonson seems to have found people ready enough, in the words of the Epilogue, to 'tax the maker of self-love'. The presentation of Horace in *Poetaster* is more subtle, for he is shown as a lesser poet at the court of Augustus than Virgil, and is subjected to some mockery within the play, as when Tucca characterizes him, in a phrase echoing Cordatus's description of Carlo Buffone, as one who 'will sooner lose his best friend than his least jest' (IV.iii.110).[1] At the same time, Horace plainly speaks for Jonson, and he laid himself open, as his 'Apologetical Dialogue', published with the play, shows, to the criticism that he attacked:

The Law and Lawyers, Captains and the Players,
By their particular names.

(1.82)

---

[1] Compare *Every Man Out of his Humour*, Induction, p. 359, 'he will sooner lose his soul than a jest and prophane even the most holy things, to excite laughter'.

It is ironical that Horace's theme in the play is that the true satirist should tax the vice, not the person.

In relation to the development of satire in drama, these plays go beyond *Every Man out of his Humour* in one important respect, in their attempt to link bad writing with vice. So when Crispinus (Marston) is given a purge at the end of *Poetaster* to cleanse him of hard words, his restoration to health requires also careful study of good authors, which will bring him to a condition of moral health, rejecting

> the discords of those jangling rhymers,
> That with their bad and scandalous practices
> Bring all true arts and learning in contempt.
>
> (V.iii.616)

In attacking bad poets, Jonson mocks their wretched verses by imitating them; Horace and Virgil recite passages from their own poems to show what poetry ought to be, while Crispinus and Demetrius are mocked in parodies of the styles of Marston and Dekker. The bad taste of Tucca is also displayed when he makes his boy-followers act out the sort of dialogue he likes, exaggerating the ranting strain of Greene, Kyd and Marlowe, as they shout in 'King Darius' doleful strain':

> O doleful days! O direful deadly dump!
> O wicked world! and worldly wickedness!
>
> (III.iv.210)

In doing this, Jonson seems to have introduced into English a sense of conscious plagiarism and conscious parody. In this play, Crispinus offers a song which Tibullus realizes is 'all borrowed; 'tis Horace's: hang him, plagiary!' (IV.iii.95). In the revised version of *Every Man in his Humour*, prepared possibly as late as about 1612, possibly earlier, Jonson makes a significant small alteration in the final scene, by having the gull Matheo-Matthew parody, not merely imitate, the verses of Samuel Daniel. In the first version, Matheo lifts his lines 'out of a book, called Delia' (V.iii.289), whereas in the revision, he garbles them, so that Knowell cries out, 'A *Parody*! A *parody*! with a kind of miraculous gift, to make it absurder than it was' (V.v.26). In the *Oxford English Dictionary* Jonson is cited as the first to use both of these words in English.

I am, of course, well aware that Jonson did not invent parody, and that examples of it and of burlesque may be found in the drama, as in other literature, before this period; but his conscious effort to find ways of using satiric techniques in drama, and his introduction of the term 'parody', reflect a serious dramatist's concern with formal problems, and show him in many respects giving his fellow-dramatists a lead. At the same time other dramatists were experimenting, notably John Marston, who turned from the writing of formal verse satires to writing plays for the new company of children at Paul's late in 1599. At first the children seem to have revived 'musty fopperies of antiquity', morality-type plays, or plays in the mode of Lyly, such as had been in the repertory of the children's companies of the 1580s. These did not please, but they may have suggested possibilities of entertainment through parody to Marston, who included burlesque of old kinds of plays in *Jack Drum's Entertainment* and in *Histriomastix*. In the latter play a wretched company of adult actors is depicted in Sir Oliver Owlet's Men, who apparently perform in a rampum-scampum style, and whose repertoire, apart from the excerpt of dismal dialogue they play from a 'Troilus and Cressida', includes such items as 'Mother Gurton's Needle'. These two plays are of uncertain date, and even more uncertain tone and quality, but belong roughly to the same period as *Antonio and Mellida* (1599/1600), in which Marston began to find a mode of his own. In this play a serious theme has been discerned, or at any rate a serious intention to display the 'ironies of a complex human situation':[1]

[Marston's] vision of life . . . was one which stressed the incapacity of any single attitude to sustain itself against the bitter ironies of incessant betrayal. . . . Marston saw the world

[1] Citing G. K. Hunter's Introduction to his edition of *Antonio and Mellida* (Regents Renaissance Drama Series, 1965), p. xiv. This is a fine and incisive critical essay, although in his enthusiasm for his own case, Hunter misrepresents the arguments of Antony Caputi in *John Marston, Satirist* (Ithaca, 1961), and of my essay, 'John Marston's Fantastical Plays: *Antonio and Mellida* and *Antonio's Revenge*', *Philological Quarterly*, XLI (Studies in English Drama presented to Baldwin Maxwell, 1962), 229-39. I have been partly persuaded by Hunter, but I think he does less than justice to the comic aspects of the play, and while my account of it owes something to his work, and that of Caputi, it differs from theirs in many respects.

as a place where nobility is forever lapsing into caricature, and communication forever betraying intention.[1]

Such a vision may underlie the play, but it is not what the play itself offers; Marston dedicates to 'Nobody' this 'worthless present of my slighter idleness', and a description of the action would make it sound like 'a repetitive farrago of all the silliest elements known to Elizabethan drama'.[2] Rather than seeking to explain the way in which 'characters veer from insensate stupidity to diabolical cunning without warning and apparently without cause; attitudes are assumed and dropped at the merest whim of the author; situations are laboriously built up and then abandoned' by supposing that Marston's 'real interests lay elsewhere',[3] it is worth considering whether his dramatic purpose is revealed by just these aspects of the play.

For in *Antonio and Mellida* Marston does not just include many of 'the silliest elements known to Elizabethan drama', but uses these consciously to create particular effects. The discontinuities of the action, and abrupt changes in character, work in part at least to expose the absurdities of a variety of dramatic clichés suggestive usually of the now outmoded drama played by the adult companies some years previously. The play is written with a deliberate self-consciousness, as the Induction establishes, in which the child-actors compare notes about their parts, and what humours they are to display. Antonio, the hero as the title indicates, announces that he must 'take this feigned presence of an Amazon, calling myself Florizel and I know not what. I a voice to play a lady! I shall ne'er do it.' The action opens with Antonio, apparently cast on shore after a sea-battle in which he thinks his father Andrugio has been killed, lamenting his fortunes, and calling for death, in a speech of fine rant:

Heart, wilt not break? And thou, abhorred life,
Wilt thou still breathe in my enraged blood?

The images swell with the horror of 'reeking gore', and fanciful hyperboles:

Could not the fretting sea
Have roll'd me up in wrinkles of his brow?

(I.i.23)

---

[1] Hunter's *Antonio and Mellida*, p. xviii.   [2] *Ibid.*, p. xii.   [3] *Ibid.*, p. xii.

Yet all this while we are conscious of the boy-actor, perhaps with a breaking voice, delivering these lines in the improbable disguise of an Amazon. How he comes to be in this disguise is not explained, and the grand speech leads nowhere, for instead of seeking death, he ends by thinking of his 'adored Mellida'. A little later, Antonio sees Mellida approaching with the court ladies, and cries out again in passionate strain:

> O now, Antonio, press thy spirit forth
> In following passion, knit thy senses close,
> Heap up thy powers, double all thy man.

(I.i.158)

The 'passion' proves pointless, however, for Mellida and the rest calmly accept Antonio as a 'sweet beauty', a woman, and the scene closes with Rossaline taking her new-found friend off:

> Sweet lady! Nay, good sweet! Now, by my troth,
> We'll be bedfellows.

(I.i.256)

Nothing more is heard of their being 'bedfellows', and the possibilities for embarrassment or discovery in the situation are not developed. The presentation of Antonio in these scenes is typical. Passionate speeches evaporate into silence, or inactivity, and four times in the play Antonio 'falls to the ground' according to the stage directions, at moments when some strong action might be looked for. The action moves in unexpected twists and comic juxtapositions; the characters do not so much inhabit roles as adopt conscious poses which they can drop and change at the author's will; and continually there is a sense of mocking reference to a range of dramatic conventions, and of the exploitation of the boys as aping adults. Characters may, so to speak, write their speeches as they deliver them, as when Antonio addresses Mellida:

> and thou and I will live –
> Let's think like what – and thou and I will live
> Like unmatch'd mirrors of calamity.

(III.i.295)

Sometimes characters step out of their parts to comment directly on the action, as when Antonio, at last penetrating Mellida's disguise in IV.i, bursts into Italian, and the two lovers freeze for twenty lines into conventional sonneteering postures, pouring out their passion in florid Italian; the Page who is with them remains behind to comment to 'the auditors', 'I think confusion of Babel is fall'n upon these lovers'. In the Induction an actor in the person of Alberto tells us that he will also be playing Andrugio, who first appears in Act III; there comes a point where Alberto must vanish to enable Andrugio to return, and in V.i. Alberto suddenly accepts the advice of Feliche that he abandon his fruitless pursuit of Rossaline, and commit suicide. He goes off with a farewell to Feliche and to the audience:

> Farewell, dear friend, expect no more of me;
> Here ends my part in this love's comedy.

Alberto is one of a group of affected courtiers among the 'thirty-nine servants and my monkey – that makes the fortieth' (V.ii.52) who serve Rossaline, and who exist in the play to display their humours in comic contrast to the passion of Antonio and Mellida. Lurking in the court too is Feliche, a character who presents himself in the Induction as an Asper figure, and who has some fine speeches such as might become the spokesman of a formal verse satire; but after delivering two sharp attacks on envy in III.ii, he is immediately shown as bursting with self-pity and envy of Castilio's apparent success with the ladies. Everything is mocked, in inconsequential action and dialogue contained within an absurd fiction. This is not to say that serious values and serious drama are attacked; the exaggeration, amounting often to caricature, of all stances, the heroic, the passionate, the stoic, the tragic, the amorous, distance these, and make us see them objectively, acted by boys aping adults self-consciously, and continually reminding the audience of Seneca, Kyd, Shakespeare, Sidney's *Arcadia*, and other literary representatives of this or that attitude. Here the sense of parody of familiar literary conventions and stances is very strong, and Marston seems to have taken the idea of satiric drama in a different direction from that of Jonson, but one perhaps as interesting and important.

If Jonson developed in a powerful way the possibilities latent for drama in the variety of satirical spokesman implicit in formal verse satire, Marston saw how to exploit the child-actors in a new kind of comedy mocking adult conventions, and then in turn mocking the mockers. His characters are 'puppets who are completely unaware of themselves',[1] but played by actors who remain conscious of themselves as posing in roles, and managed by a dramatist who takes care to remind his audience of the game he is playing. The effect is hilarious, but not destructive, and Marston shows how to use and maintain the detachment of the audience from the action. If he had serious ethical aims, then I think in this play they dissolve in the comedy; but however that may be, *Antonio and Mellida* is a delightful and successful play in another sense, in finding a new way of exploiting satire. It was also, in itself, something of a dead end, in that its particular vein of mockery could hardly be repeated, and Marston went on to experiment with other conventions, those of revenge tragedy, in *Antonio's Revenge*. Between them Jonson and Marston developed new potentialities for comedy, by seeing how to make dramatic use of formal verse satire, and how to win advantages from the very limitations of the boy-actors.

(iv) *Troilus and Cressida*

Troilus and Cressida has provoked more critical disagreement than the other 'dark' comedies. This play, probably the first of them to be written, as the Stationers' Register entry of February 1603 would suggest a date of composition not later than 1602, is the closest of them in date to the new comedies of Jonson and Marston. The uncertain evidence provided by the title-pages of the quarto, the epistle to the reader in the second issue, and the placing of it in the First Folio of 1623, allow no conclusions to be drawn as to when, where and how it was originally performed; but the writer of the epistle, who may be regarded as the first critic of the play, had no doubt that it was one of the best of Shakespeare's comedies: 'amongst all there is none more witty than this'. The stage-history of the play is almost a blank until the twentieth century, and it has won its place in the repertories of the major Shakespeare companies since the First World War. The critics too have developed a passionate interest in the play in this century, discovering, in

---

[1] Hunter's *Antonio and Mellida*, p. xv.

D

the wake of Bernard Shaw,[1] how 'modern' the play is, as it may seem to relate to the futility of two world wars, or the confusions of present-day politicians. So recently Jan Kott, finding it a play more cruel than tragedy, and describing it as 'a dispute about the existence of a moral order in a cruel and irrational world', headed his chapter on it 'Amazing and Modern'.[2] In a serious age we find our seriousness reflected in Shakespeare, and it is not surprising that many critics, most recently Northrop Frye, have succeeded in reading the play as 'essentially a tragedy'.[3]

Plays which balance on the knife-edge of satire are especially liable to thematic and tonal misreadings, but attention to the dramatic shape and context of *Troilus and Cressida* confirms the view of the commentator in the quarto that it is 'passing full of the palm comical'. It is to simplify too crudely to suppose that Shakespeare wrote this play directly within a convention of 'comical satire' as established by Jonson,[4] but it does seem clear that he learned much from Jonson and Marston, using techniques they had developed in a rich and subtle expansion of the satirical mode. So Shakespeare plays his own variations on the satirical figures invented by Jonson: Asper, the just man, truly evaluating men and their actions, becomes Ulysses, but with the difference that he has a place in the action, and his assertion of authority as a wise man is undermined continually by the expediency of his actions; Carlo Buffone is translated into Thersites; and the pretender to virtue, Macilente, who is contaminated by his own envy, and so becomes something of a malcontent, may be detected in Achilles, and perhaps, more comically treated, in Ajax. The new techniques of Marston are also exploited in *Troilus and Cressida*. The whole play carries an element of general parody in relation to the grand Homeric legend of the Trojan war, as the heroes of that are displayed in

[1] See his Preface to *Plays Unpleasant* (1898), p. xxi. Dryden's version of the play held the stage in the eighteenth century, and Shakespeare's *Troilus and Cressida* had to wait until 1907 for a London revival.
[2] *Shakespeare Our Contemporary* (1964), p. 62.
[3] See *Fools of Time. Studies in Shakespearean Tragedy* (Toronto, 1967), pp. 47-8. The phrase 'essentially a tragedy' is taken from William Toole's unsatisfactory book, *Shakespeare's Problem Plays* (The Hague, 1966), p. 202.
[4] As claimed by O. J. Campbell in *Comicall Satyre and Shakespeare's 'Troilus and Cressida'*, pp. 185ff.

the fumbling and insecure postures of Shakespeare's characters. Like Marston in *Antonio and Mellida*, Shakespeare also here establishes and exploits a dislocation of character from role, and a discontinuity between speech and action in, for example, the presentation of Ajax, or of Troilus, whose grand rhetoric as lover is comically exploded by the matter-of-fact practicality of Pandarus – he wishes, so to speak, to play Romeo, but neither his character nor the action sustain him in this role, and the effect is satiric.

By such means Shakespeare maintains throughout the play a note of satiric detachment; no character is allowed to win sufficient prominence or sympathy to dominate the stage, and the whole action is built up by ironic juxtapositioning and comic counterpointing, and punctuated by the satiric commentary of Thersites. In concentrating on the structure and tonality of the play in what follows, I shall comment only indirectly on some important aspects of its themes and ideas, which have been much discussed in a general way; I mean, for example, that clash of values which may be seen thematically as a conflict between politics, represented by the Greeks, and ethics, represented by the Trojans, and which is developed more subtly in terms of clashes within the Greek position between the grand theories enunciated by Ulysses and others, and the cheap tricks tried out on Achilles. Within the Trojan position too there is a clash between ideals of heroism and honour, and the practical application of these in action. I shall also say little about the important contrasts between perspectives of time in the play – the contrast between that sense of the immediate compulsions of practical life – as these demand fighting, or the sudden return of Cressida to the Greeks in the shadow of the comment by Paris, 'There is no help; the bitter disposition of the time will have it so' (IV.i.50) – and that eternity to which Cressida appeals in swearing to be true:

> When time is old and hath forgot itself,
> When waterdrops have worn the stones of Troy,
> And blind oblivion swallow'd cities up. . .

> (III.ii.181)

This concern with time is especially important in *Troilus and Cressida* because so many of the characters have an existence independent of the play, as their names evoke the heroic values associated with the *Iliad*, and the legend of Troy as this has filtered through the imagination of Europe. Shakespeare consciously plays off Pandarus, Troilus and Cressida against our knowledge of what their names stand for in III.ii, when they join together to cry, in Pandar's words, 'let all constant men be Troiluses, all false women Cressids, and all brokers-between Pandars' (III.ii.198); but the legend carries through to us also the idea of Helen as the most beautiful woman in the world, of Hector and Achilles as great heroes, and so on. The action of the play is measured in part against this larger consciousness possessed by the audience.[1]

Within the action there are three strands which interweave to create the pattern and tonality of the play, and which culminate in what is perhaps the most curious feature of *Troilus and Cressida*, its three endings. These strands are set off against one another, and contain within themselves discontinuities and sardonic juxtapositions which affect sooner or later the stance taken by each of the main characters. The first and perhaps most obvious strand is the heroic, for the prologue promises a play about war, whatever the title suggests. He comes on stage 'suited In like condition as our argument', which is to say in armour, to inform us that the play begins in the middle of 'these broils' of the siege of Troy:

> Like or find fault, do as your pleasures are:
> Now good or bad, 'tis but the chance of war.

In this war action, or rather heroic action, for no battle takes place until the last act, Hector comes nearest to being the model for a tragic hero. He comes near enough for our discomfort, but there is a final discontinuity or incongruity between character and role in the presentation of him. He is praised on all sides for his virtue and nobility, from the moment when he is seen returning from the battlefield in I.ii; and this nobility is seen in action when he brings the single combat with Ajax to an end to praise his adversary, and when later he has Achilles at his

---

[1] For further discussion of this point, see my essay '*Troilus and Cressida* Reconsidered', *University of Toronto Quarterly*, XXXII (1963), 142-54. This was reprinted in the Signet edition of the play (edited by Daniel Seltzer, 1963), pp. 265-81.

mercy and lets him go (V.vi). This is the Hector described by
Nestor:

> And I have seen thee,
> As hot as Perseus, spur thy Phrygian steed,
> Despising many forfeits and subduements,
> When thou hast hung thy advanced sword i'th'air,
> Not letting it decline on the declin'd,
> That I have said to some my standers-by
> 'Lo, Jupiter is yonder, dealing life!'

(IV.v.185)

This chivalric Hector, a godlike figure, deals life rather than
death even on the battlefield. The image is not sustained,
however, throughout the play; it is tarnished in the Trojan
council scene, where Hector's idea of honour is seen to dwell in
fame and reputation rather than in morality. Knowing it is
wrong for the Trojans to keep the stolen Helen, he yet proposes
to retain her:

> For 'tis a cause that hath no mean dependence
> Upon our joint and several dignities.

(II.ii.192)

He has indeed already at this point sent his challenge to the
Greeks, claiming:

> He hath a lady wiser, fairer, truer,
> Than ever Greek did couple in his arms,

(I.iii.275)

so that the outcome of the debate among the Trojan princes is
in a sense already settled. Hector agrees with Troilus in effect
that Helen is 'a theme of honour and renown', but it is both a
comic and harsh irony in the play that Hector alone fights for
his mistress. Helen is seen holding back Paris from the battle,
as Troilus appears in I.i rendered unable to fight because of the
'cruel battle' Cressida has brought about in his heart, and Achilles
denies even Hector's appeal to him to engage in battle in order
to keep a pledge made to his mistress Polyxena (V.i.40). The
direct influence these themes of honour and renown have is to
keep men from heroic activity, except in so far as Diomedes
may be said to fight for Cressida when he wears her sleeve on
his helm, but by that time (V.iv) she has become a theme of

spite and revenge, not honour. Hector, by contrast, who
challenges the Greeks in praise of Andromache, and fights with
Ajax on her account, and who is the only figure in the play
shown with a faithful wife, rejects her advice at the end, and
goes to battle when she would have him stay. His heroic stance
here, when he refuses to behave like Troilus and Achilles, and
allow himself to be distracted from fighting by a woman, is
undercut by our sense of his lack of wisdom in ignoring
Andromache's prophetic powers. In his final weariness, he
finds strength to hunt down a Greek merely to win a 'sumptuous
armour':

> Wilt thou not, beast, abide?
> Why then, fly on, I'll hunt thee for thy hide.

(V.vi.30)

Here Hector repudiates all that Nestor found in him, and in
pursuit of 'honour' becomes a hunter after his kill, a mere
butcher, and no better than the myrmidons of Achilles, who
hunt him in turn.

It is hardly necessary to emphasize that Achilles, who, unlike
the Homeric figure, has his followers slaughter the unarmed
Hector, is still further from the idea of a hero. This is brought
out in the confrontation of Achilles and Ulysses in III.iii, where
Ulysses appeals to him to return to the battlefield and fight.
The appeal is couched in terms Ulysses thinks Achilles will
understand:

> Take the instant way;
> For honour travels in a strait so narrow
> Where one but goes abreast. Keep then the path;
> For emulation hath a thousand sons
> That one by one pursue; if you give way,
> Or hedge aside from the direct forthright,
> Like to an enter'd tide they all rush by,
> And leave you hindmost.

(III.iii.153)

Here the reasons Ulysses the politician gives for Achilles to
fight reduce the idea of martial glory to joining the rat-race,
or keeping abreast of fashion: 'The present eye praises the
present object'. In this view ideals and principles go by the
board, and honour is tied to 'emulation', or being competitive.

Achilles is prompted by Ulysses to think, like Hector, of his reputation, but in a more narrow way:

> I see my reputation is at stake,
> My fame is shrewdly gor'd.

(III.iii.227)

In any case, neither 'honour', nor 'reputation', nor even a direct rebuke from Hector:

> I pray you, let us see you in the field;
> We have had pelting wars since you refus'd
> The Grecians' cause,

(IV.v.266)

brings Achilles to the field. His oath to his mistress Polyxena is more important to him than all these:

> honour or go or stay,
> My major vow lies here.

(V.i.41)

It takes the death of Patroclus, his 'masculine whore', if we can believe Thersites' description, to arouse him finally, and in Achilles there is no sense even of the possible grandeur of Hector. Indeed, he may be seen in a different relation to Jonson's humour figures from that suggested earlier, not as a distant relation of Macilente, but as standing to Asper-Ulysses like one of Jonson's humour characters; Ulysses endeavours to bring Achilles out of his humour of surly pride, and only succeeds in bringing Ajax into the same condition:

> They set me up, in policy, that mongrel cur, Ajax, against that
> dog of as bad a kind, Achilles; and now is the cur Ajax
> prouder than the cur Achilles, and will not arm to-day. . . .

(V.iv.15)

Troilus, the third possible hero, fights or refuses to fight according to his mood. Like Achilles, he has no loyalties larger than those to his mistress, and reduces the war to personal terms. When he sees Cressida in the arms of Diomedes, his reaction is characteristic – he will hate Diomedes, and pursue him on the battlefield, without regard to anything else:

> As much as I do Cressid love,
> So much by weight hate I her Diomed.

That sleeve is mine that he'll bear on his helm;
Were it a casque compos'd by Vulcan's skill,
My sword should bite it.

(V.ii.165)

At the end, too, he thinks only of personal revenge for the death of Hector, transferring his hate to Achilles:

And, thou great-siz'd coward,
No space of earth shall sunder our two hates.
I'll haunt thee like a wicked conscience still.

(V.x.26)

The chivalric ideals Hector seems to stand for crumble into nothing in the violence of battle. The conduct of all three characters, Hector, Achilles and Troilus, is framed by two perspectives on honour or reputation. One is that of Ulysses, the apparent Asper-figure, whose wisdom is seen in fact to be confined within the limits of the practical politician, and revealed as in its way petty. In his advice to Achilles he urges:

let not virtue seek
Remuneration for the thing it was;
For beauty, wit,
High birth, vigour of bone, desert in service,
Love, friendship, charity, are subjects all
To envious and calumniating Time.

(III.iii.169)

If this were true, there would be little point in bothering about 'honour' at all, or anything touching upon an idea of 'virtue', unless they brought immediate returns in the form of 'remuneration'. To Troilus, by contrast, Helen

is a theme of honour and renown,
A spur to valiant and magnanimous deeds,
Whose present courage may beat down our foes,
And fame in time to come canonize us.

(II.ii.199)

This is Troilus speaking in the full flow of his romantic ardour in the first part of the play, and thinking of fame as possibly enshrining his reputation in perpetuity; but, having this sense of 'renown', he throws it away in the reckless pursuit of revenge, first upon Diomedes, and then upon Achilles, losing sight of honour and magnanimity. Ulysses debases values and ideals for the immediate political gains he hopes to make, and Troilus sacrifices them in a personal vendetta.

A second strand in the action is that indicated by the play's title, and has to do with love. Troilus appears in the opening scene as a courtly lover absorbed in the war within his heart rather than the Trojan war; Helen may be a theme of 'honour and renown' to him, but Cressida is not, as she prompts him to disarm rather than inspiring him to noble deeds:

Call here my varlet; I'll unarm again.

This opening line follows on a prologue promising a play about war, and already begins to suggest the degree to which Troilus's 'love' is in fact a passion, comparable in its romantic exaggeration and rejection of reason with his devotion to 'honour' in the Trojan council scene later. He confesses as much when he says to Pandarus:

> I tell thee I am mad
In Cressid's love.

(I.i.50)

In this scene Troilus recalls Antonio in Marston's *Antonio and Mellida*, in that he seems set on acting out the role of romantic lover, and reminds himself of the proper mental attitude when his attention wanders for a moment:[1]

At Priam's royal table do I sit,
And when fair Cressid comes into my thoughts –
So, traitor! – 'When she comes!' – When is she thence?

(I.i.29)

A discontinuity is set up between the hyperboles of Troilus and the actual state of affairs; he cries out:

Tell me, Apollo, for thy Daphne's love
What Cressid is, what Pandar, and what we?
Her bed is India, there she lies, a pearl;
Between our Ilium and where she resides
Let it be call'd the wild and wand'ring flood;
Ourself the merchant, and this sailing Pandar
Our doubtful hope, our convoy, and our bark.

(I.i.97)

[1] The last line is Rowe's generally accepted emendation of the Quarto and Folio reading 'then she comes when she is thence', which makes no sense.

Here Troilus is, so to speak, writing his own speeches, and expanding his images as he talks, 'Let it be called . . .'; he does not do it very well, for the idea of a merchant buying a pearl, though it represents what in fact he is doing, contradicts the posture of romantic ardour. In any case, it is placed by its contrast with the language of Pandarus, and his image of manipulating the affair of Troilus and Cressida as if he were making a cake. The stance of Troilus contrasts also with the bawdy and flippancy of Cressida in I.ii, where she jests about him, with her 'What sneaking fellow comes yonder?', and calls Pandarus what in fact he is, a bawd (I.ii.273). Troilus's speeches do not issue in action, but leave him, like Antonio, prostrate, and when he goes off eventually at the end of I.i to fight, it is not for love of Cressida, or for loyalty to Troy, but only because Aeneas sufficiently distracts his attention from Cressida to draw him to the 'good sport' on the field of battle.

The romantic ardours of Troilus and his pose as lover bear little relation to what he really intends to do, namely to seduce Cressida. Both the passion and the intention are real and convincing, but we are aware, as Troilus is not, of the disconnection between them, which satirically places him, and makes him at times a comic figure. Cressida's love for him is just as 'real', and convincing, as it is expressed in her rhyming soliloquy at the end of I.ii; here the couplets following on a scene in prose, and the stance of Cressida confiding in the audience, are reminiscent of Beatrice bursting into quatrains when she confesses to the audience her love for Benedick in *Much Ado about Nothing*, III.i, or Helena confirming her determination to win Bertram at the end of the opening scene in *All's Well that Ends Well*. Here she drops her flippancy to be earnest for a moment:

> more in Troilus thousandfold I see
> Than in the glass of Pandar's praise may be.
> Yet hold I off.

(I.ii.276)

In the context of this, her flippancy and wit in conversing with Pandarus are a means of defence against his pressure on her to yield to Troilus; and yet at the same time her readiness to engage in bawdy talk shows her familiarity in word and thought, if not in deed, with what he would bring her to do.

One model Troilus and Cressida have for their 'love' is shown in III.i, the only scene in which Helen appears, jesting, as Cressida had done, with Pandarus, and preventing Paris from fighting, 'I would fain have arm'd today, but my Nell would not have it so' (III.i.128). The dialogue here conveys a heavy sensual atmosphere. Pandarus enters to ask Paris to make excuses on behalf of Troilus, who will be supping with Cressida, not at court, and he at first mistakes the witty Servant's description of Helen as 'the mortal Venus, the heart-blood of beauty, love's invisible soul' (III.i.30) for a comment on Cressida. Helen teases him, caresses him, distracts him from his business by continual interruptions, enforcing perhaps the quibble on 'quean' in his words as he tries to disengage himself, 'Sweet queen, sweet queen, there's a sweet queen i'faith. . . . What says my sweet queen, my very very sweet queen?', and so on. She presumably returns to the embraces of Paris as they make him sing his song, 'Love, love, nothing but love . . .'; but the love in this scene is nothing more than 'hot blood, hot thoughts, and hot deeds', in the words of Pandarus, echoing Paris (III.i.125). The scene is gay and amusing, but the court of Troy is transmuted through this dialogue into a kind of high-class brothel, and love becomes another word for lechery.

This has an important bearing on what immediately follows, the coming together of Troilus and Cressida, brought to bed by Pandarus in III.ii to swear eternal loyalty and truth to one another, when on one level they are acting out another brothel scene. Their passion is real enough, conveyed in Troilus's hyperboles, and in Cressida's image of her loss of control:

> I love you now, but till now not so much
> But I might master it. In faith, I lie.
> My thoughts were like unbridled children, grown
> Too headstrong for their mother.

> (III.ii.117)

However, they do not realize how easily that love may become merely 'hot deeds'. The night over, Cressida is forced to go to the Greek camp in exchange for Antenor, and notoriously allows herself to be kissed by all the Greek warriors after Agamemnon has saluted her in this way; only Ulysses remains aloof, and provides a savage comment:

Fie, fie upon her!
There's language in her eye, her cheek, her lip,
Nay, her foot speaks; her wanton spirits look out
At every joint and motive of her body.
O, these encounterers, so glib of tongue,
That gives accosting welcome ere it comes,
And wide unclasp the table of their thoughts
To every ticklish reader! Set them down
For sluttish spoils of opportunity
And daughters of the game.

(IV.v.54)

This is not a sudden transformation in her; from the beginning
her language has been 'wanton', and Troilus has made her
wanton in act. What she becomes is a reflection upon him as
much as upon her, and reveals the distance between his 'honour'
and 'love' as expressed in his romantic hyperboles, and a proper
sense of values. In spite of the fine language, his love is on one
level mere lechery; he has made Cressida his mistress, and if
he could do it, why should not others? As for her, she follows
the fashion of Helen and Paris, or Polyxena and Achilles, but
especially that of Helen, with whom she is linked in III.i as 'the
mortal Venus, the heart-blood of beauty', and whose example
she emulates, in adapting herself to her 'captor', Diomedes, as
Helen has adapted herself to Paris. It is fitting that Troilus's
love turns to spite against Diomedes, for the 'truth' he urges on
Cressida before they part in IV.iv was no part of the initial
seduction or compact with her.

A third strand in the action consists of the satiric and comic
elements, focused primarily in the trick practised on 'blockish
Ajax' in II.iii, and in the activities of Pandarus and Thersites.
The sense in which Pandarus remains a detached observer and
intriguer, contriving to bring Troilus and Cressida together as
much for his pleasure as theirs, acting as voyeur and bawd, is
important for establishing a critical perspective on this affair of
'love'. Thersites, who combines something of the malice of
Macilente and the scurrility of Carlo Buffone, provides a sardonic chorus, which carries some weight, 'all the argument
is a whore and a cuckold' (II.iii.68). Again, his comments
accentuate the critical detachment with which the central
figures are displayed. Pandarus seems to have little idea of

love except in terms of sex, 'hot thoughts and hot deeds'; and Thersites hardly conceives the possibility of love or loyalty, or heroism, so that neither of them can be trusted as a commentator, for their perspectives are evidently too limited. They command a degree of assent since what they say is in part borne out by the undercurrent of self-exposure in the presentation of the main participants in the play's action.

This undercurrent emerges in moments of splendid comedy, as, for instance, notably in the Greek council scene. There the great generals reveal themselves as wordy politicians grinding out parliamentary platitudes, and after their grand statements concerning the 'specialty of rule', they notoriously resort to a cheap trick to bring the sulking Achilles back on to the battlefield. Their rhetoric is exploded nicely on the arrival of Aeneas, bringing Hector's challenge from Troy. For all the talk of 'degree' in the council has turned on the proposition that Agamemnon,

> Thou great commander, nerve and bone of Greece,
> Heart of our numbers, soul and only spirit
> In whom the tempers and the minds of all
> Should be shut up,
>
> (I.iii.55)

ought to be obeyed, in effect, as king; moreover, the language of Nestor and Ulysses suggests that the stature and regality of Agamemnon are self-evident, for they address him continually as 'Great Agamemnon', and Nestor humbles himself in his opening words:

> With due observance of thy godlike seat,
> Great Agamemnon, Nestor shall apply
> Thy latest words.
>
> (I.iii.31)

Whether 'seat' here means literally 'throne', or figuratively 'authority', makes little difference to the comic effect of the entry of Aeneas, who is either unable or unwilling to recognize this 'god in office':

> How may
> A stranger to those most imperial looks
> Know them from eyes of other mortals?

Agamemnon	How?
Aeneas	Aye.

> I ask that I might waken reverence,
> And bid the cheek be ready with a blush
> Modest as morning when she coldly eyes
> The youthful Phoebus.
> Which is that god in office, guiding men?
> Which is the high and mighty Agamemnon?

(I.iii.223)

The words and actions of Achilles, Patroclus and Ajax are at times close enough to the parodies of them by Thersites to speak home to us, and Ajax is made a general comic butt in his readiness to accept all praise. On the Trojan side, the affair of Troilus is kept at a level of witty detachment not only in the perspective Pandarus provides of it, but also in the self-exposure of Troilus, for the distance between his idealization of love and the reality of lust is made amusing as well as poignant. At the very moment when they are about to come together, he is borne off in imagination:

> I stalk about her door,
> Like a strange soul upon the Stygian banks
> Staying for waftage. O, be thou my Charon,
> And give me swift transportation to those fields
> Where I may wallow in the lily beds
> Proposed for the deserver! O gentle Pandar,
> From Cupid's shoulder pluck his painted wings,
> And fly with me to Cressid!

(III.ii.7)

This echoes Troilus's first image of her, as a pearl in India (I.i.99), but with a deeper resonance, for he equates going to Cressida with a visit to the underworld, confusing the realm of Hades with perhaps the Elysian fields, and echoing the Song of Solomon, with an added note of sensuality in the word 'wallow'; at the same time, his stance here is made comic by the matter-of-fact rejoinder of Pandarus, 'Walk here i'th'orchard; I'll bring her straight', for Cressida is, of course, close by him. Pandarus, who hovers about the lovers in this scene, vicariously enjoys the sexual activities of others; he bustles about his comic business as a bawd, mocked by Cressida, by Helen and her Servant, and playing the fool to them.

This thread of humour, mockery and at times near-farce diminishes in the later part of the play, but even there is sustained in the commentary of Thersites. Often he is played on stage, and treated in discussions of the play, as if the boils, plagues and diseases he wishes upon others afflicted him, that is to say, as a character foul in body and in mind. There is nothing in the text to support the image of a syphilitic, filthy figure, clothed in rags, and covered in open sores, such as was seen in the 1968 Royal Shakespeare Company production; the diseases are of his imagination, and colour his view of things. To Achilles he is a fool, and has a fool's licence to speak out. When he first appears, interrupting a quarrel between Ajax and Thersites, Achilles says to Ajax, 'Will you set your wit to a fool's?' (II.i.83), implying that it is the function of Thersites to be witty. Later on Thersites sets out to prove Agamemnon, Achilles, and Patroclus are all fools, and when Patroclus would intervene, Achilles stays him:

Achilles	He is a privileg'd man. Proceed, Thersites.
Thersites	Agamemnon is a fool; Achilles is a fool; Thersites is a fool; and, as aforesaid, Patroclus is a fool.
Achilles	Derive this; come.
Thersites	Agamemnon is a fool to offer to command Achilles; Achilles is a fool to be commanded of Agamemnon; Thersites is a fool to serve such a fool; and Patroclus is a fool positive.
Patroclus	Why am I a fool?
Thersites	Make that demand of the Creator. It suffices me thou art.

(II.iii.54)

Here Thersites is seen as a licensed fool, riddling upon the meanings of 'fool', and proving his superiors to be fools much as Feste in *Twelfth Night*, I.v, and the Fool in *King Lear*, I.iv, demonstrate Olivia and Lear to be the real 'fools'. Thersites differs from these as Carlo Buffone differs from them, for he is both malicious and scurrilous; and yet the sense in which he has the role of fool may help to bring out the links between him and Pandarus, who plays 'fool' for the Trojans. In many ways they are complementary to one another; both are outsiders in

their society, whose occupation is to observe the 'pretty encounters' of others in love and war. Pandarus enjoys watching
the Trojan heroes return from battle in I.ii, hacked and bloodied,
while at the end, Thersites dodges about the battlefield entertaining himself with the spectacle of others fighting. As Pandarus
gets his pleasure in bringing together Troilus and Cressida, and
watching them make love, so Thersites finds satisfaction in
spying on Diomedes and Cressida;

> . . . the sun borrows of the moon when Diomed keeps his
> word. I will rather leave to see Hector than not to dog him.
> They say he keeps a Trojan drab and uses the traitor Calchas'
> tent; I'll after. Nothing but lechery! All incontinent varlets!
>
> (V.i.90)

The difference is that where Pandarus is soft, indulgent, and
sees nothing wrong, Thersites is hard, pitiless, and sees nothing
right; but the moral disease which prevents our taking either
of them very seriously is the same, a kind of voyeurism, as they
obtain excitement and gratification in watching, not in doing.
This disease manifests itself in different ways, as Pandarus
dwindles into a bawd, and Thersites loses himself in the labyrinth of his fury and the venom of 'spiteful execrations' (II.iii.8).

The effect of the interlacing of these three strands in the
action is to maintain in us a sense of detachment, an awareness
of the critical placing of the characters, and of their attitudes
to love, war and honour. It is fitting that the last scene should
offer not one but three possible endings to the play, one for the
heroic action, one for the love action, and one relating to the
comic undercurrent. The first 'ending' comes with the announcement of the death of Hector, as Troilus cries out:

> Let him that will a screech-owl aye be called
> Go in to Troy and say there, 'Hector's dead';
> There is a word will Priam turn to stone,
> Make wells and Niobes of the maids and wives,
> Cold statues of the youth, and, in a word,
> Scare Troy out of itself, But march away.
> Hector is dead; there is no more to say.
>
> (V.x.16)

Here the play might stop, if it were an heroic play with Hector
as protagonist, but as the Trojans march off, Troilus halts

them, 'Stay yet', and goes on to unburden himself of his hatred
for Achilles, or Diomedes, or perhaps both:

> thou great-siz'd coward,
> No space of earth shall sunder our two hates;
> I'll haunt thee like a wicked conscience still,
> That mouldeth goblins swift as frenzy's thoughts.
> Strike a free march to Troy. With comfort go:
> Hope of revenge shall hide our inward woe.

(V.x.26)

Again the Trojans march away, on this cry for revenge which
springs characteristically from Troilus in terms of a personal
spite, and in language that recalls the 'inward woe' that brought
him to fight, the loss of Cressida. Now Pandarus enters to hold
Troilus for a moment, but to be cast off and left as comic
chorus to address the audience in a final speech.[1] At this point
Pandarus and Thersites seem in a sense to merge, as Pandarus
appears physically afflicted with those diseases Thersites has so
often invoked in the play: moral disease is translated symbolic-
ally into physical aches and pains, and it is appropriate that
Pandarus should end anticipating a death soon, brought on,
apparently, by some form of venereal disease:

> Some two months hence my will shall here be made.
> It should be now, but that my fear is this,
> Some galled goose of Winchester would hiss.
> Till then I'll sweat and seek about for eases,
> And at that time bequeath you my diseases.

(V.x.51)

All three endings are fitting, in carrying through to the last
the sardonic juxtapositions offered by this play, which yields a
predominant sense of the limitations of the human situation;
the best of men, like Hector, can imagine ideals, but cannot
sustain them in action; love as conceived by Troilus becomes
lechery and leads to spite and thoughts of revenge; and Greek

---

[1] The dismissal of Pandarus is duplicated in the Folio text at the end of V.iii.
I accept Alice Walker's view (New Cambridge edition, 1957, pp. 123, 221) that
the lines as printed in V.x occupy 'the position in which Shakespeare finally
intended them to stand'. The anticipation of them in V.iii in the Folio, but not
the Quarto, text probably represents Shakespeare's first thoughts. For further
development of this point, see '*Troilus and Cressida* Reconsidered', pp. 150-4.

E

and Trojan heroes alike are mocked and contaminated by Thersites and Pandarus. *Troilus and Cressida* may be seen as the most balanced of the 'dark' comedies in achieving a successful and thorough deployment of its satirical tone, and so effecting a major purpose of satire, to expose comically and hence criticize human failings, while leaving ideals unscathed. The inadequacies of Hector and Achilles do not destroy the idea of heroism, any more than the exaggerations of Troilus damage the idea of true love; and indeed, their reputations, winnowed by the fan of time, are sturdily associated with heroism and love. But in sharply making us aware of the discrepancy between the potential and actual in human beings, that monstruosity, as Troilus says, of love, and of all else, that 'the will is infinite, and the execution confined; that the desire is boundless, and the act a slave to limit' (III.ii.78), the play works with conviction, subtlety and depth. It is a splendid play in the satirical mode, dark only in so far as it is concerned to display man not as he might be, in the heroic ideal of tragedy, or the romantic ideal of the happy comedies, but as he is, caught in that sharp comic perspective which emphasizes the discontinuities between speech and action, between principle and practice, and between the ardours of romantic love and the arrangements for effective seduction.

Troilus and Cressida was perhaps written about 1601 or 1602, and is generally considered to be the earliest of the dark comedies. It seems to be exploiting new techniques developed by Jonson and Marston more directly than the others, and is more clearly related to the growing interest in satire in the years just before it was written. In it Shakespeare could expose serious attitudes to sardonic treatment in a classical and political world relatively untroubled by Christian categories, so allowing him more freedom with clashes of tone, and in maintaining a note of satirical detachment. Moreover, he took as subject for the play only a part of one of the most 'heroic' legends of antiquity, the story of the fall of Troy, and could rely to some extent on knowledge possessed by his audience to set up a challenge to the perspective offered in the play. This is brought out at times in the play, as in vows exchanged by Troilus, Cressida and Pandarus:

> since I have taken such pains to bring you together, let all
> pitiful goers-between be called to the world's end after my name
> – call them all Pandars, let all constant men be Troiluses, all
> false women Cressids, and all brokers-between Pandars!
>
> (III.ii.196)

Helen carried the legendary status of the most beautiful woman the world had ever known, and Hector and Achilles were famed as archetypal heroes, before the play was written, and this vision of them has survived the play, modifying our attitude to it, because we see beyond the 'extant moment' and know, as Agamemnon and the other characters do not, 'What's past and what's to come' (IV.v.166). There is another way in which our external knowledge rounds out the action of a play that in one sense is bound to remain incomplete, and provides an additional note of irony, for while the play is concerned, as the Prologue tells us, with the war of Troy, it stops short at the death of Hector; we know the end, that Troy fell, and that many of the play's characters, including Achilles, Paris, and Troilus, were to die soon, so that we have the advantage over Hector and the rest of being in the position of that 'Time' to which he appeals:

> The end crowns all,
> And that old common arbitrator, Time,
> Will one day end it.
>
> (IV.v.224)

In *All's Well* and *Measure for Measure*, Shakespeare seems to experiment further, in seeking a reconciliation of comical satire with romantic comedy, and in looking for a new form which could simultaneously accommodate passion and detachment, a lightness of general tone with more than a hint of savagery. The tonality of these plays is established in large part, like that of *Troilus and Cressida*, by the vital presence of satirical figures related to those of Jonson, as Thersites and Pandarus are succeeded by Parolles and Lavache, and these give way in turn to Lucio and Pompey Bum. Discontinuities between speech and action, or character and role, such as those Marston exploited for comic theatrical effect, are used for a deeper purpose in these plays. No figures are allowed to remain enshrined in the simple perfection of a Rosalind or Viola, but heroines become perverse and full of contradictions, like Helena, singlemindedly pursuing an apparently worthless boy, or Isabella, controlling her passionate nature by a stance that is close to fanaticism; and heroes dwindle into Bertram and Angelo. The vulnerability of these figures, and of some common romantic, moral and judicial stances and commitments is matter for these plays. They differ from *Troilus and Cressida* in their 'modern' and Christian setting, suggesting a providence interested in human affairs, and envisaging the possibility of holiness as a human attribute, and of events explicable as miracles. This helps to rescue them from a position of mere satirical detachment, but also makes for difficulties of balance in them and response to them. In one respect they look back to Jonson and Marston and to Shakespeare's earlier comedies, in another they look forward to his last plays or 'romances'. Before he came to write these, however, Shakespeare's experiments in satirical comedy gave way to experiments in satirical tragedy, and these must now be considered.

3

Shakespeare
and satirical tragedy

(i) TRAGEDY FOR BOY-ACTORS AND TRAGEDY FOR ADULT ACTORS: MARSTON, JONSON AND TOURNEUR

In the sequel to *Antonio and Mellida*, *Antonio's Revenge*, Marston exploited the child-actors in a new way by mocking the conventions of heroic tragedy, with particular reference to *The Spanish Tragedy*. This play has often been regarded as a serious attempt to embody an ethical vision, a play concerned with the 'cold realities of power', a neo-stoic rendering of revenge themes, by a dramatist for whom 'evil had to be . . . a terrifying eclipse of goodness assumed to be basic', a writer 'obsessed with violence and evil'.[1] If the play has appeared something less than satisfactory, it is because Marston failed to embody his vision adequately: 'Incapable of Fletcher's frivolity, Marston approached tragedy with as serious purpose as Chapman, but he aspired to a "Senecan" ideal that was, if anything, less sophisticated than Kyd's and that equated tragic grandeur with rhetorical bombast and gruesome melo-

---

[1] The quotations are respectively from G. K. Hunter, 'English Folly and Italian Vice: The Moral Landscape of John Marston', in *Jacobean Theatre* (Stratford-upon-Avon Studies 1, edited J. R. Brown and Bernard Harris, 1960), p. 91; and from Hunter's Introduction to his edition of *Antonio's Revenge* (Regents Renaissance Drama 1965), pp. xiv, xiii.

drama.'[1] Such views seem altogether too earnest in relation to the texture of the action and dialogue. One defender of the 'serious' Marston has acutely observed two features of the play, first the detached satiric portraiture and 'philosophic stances which comment on one another, but never really engage or necessarily issue into action'; and secondly, that, 'It is one of the principal difficulties of *Antonio's Revenge* that the surface language of conventional moral concern is not merely detached from but largely contradictory of the underlying pattern of amoral ritual.'[2] Both features could be interpreted differently, as positive aspects of a satiric and mocking design, exposing to a detached and comically horrible scrutiny conventional moral concerns.

Antonio's Revenge exaggerates to the point of absurdity features of earlier revenge plays, and offers the child-actors much pompous rant and 'braggart passion' to declaim. In particular, it magnifies all the more lurid effects of *The Spanish Tragedy* from the opening scene, when Piero enters 'smear'd in blood, a poniard in one hand bloody, and a torch in the other, Strotzo following him with a cord', to the final scene, in which the conspirators 'pluck out' Piero's tongue and 'triumph over him'. The stage directions, which are presumably Marston's own, require a series of sensational effects designed to shock, like the discovery of Feliche's body hung up and 'stabb'd thick with wounds' (I.ii.193), or the revelation of the ghost of Andrugio sitting on the bed of Maria (III.ii.61). The centrepiece is the extraordinary scene in 'Saint Mark's Church' at dead of night (III.i), in which Antonio watches at the tomb of his father, sees his father's ghost rise from the tomb crying revenge and murder, and ends by stabbing the boy Julio, Piero's son, and sprinkling blood over Andrugio's tomb. He goes off crying:

> Lo, thus I heave my blood-dyed hands to heaven;
> Even like insatiate hell, still crying; 'More!
> My heart hath thirsting dropsies after gore.'
> Sound peace and rest to church, night-ghosts and graves;
> Blood cries for blood; and murder murder craves.

> (III.i.211)

---

[1] Robert Ornstein, *The Moral Vision of Jacobean Tragedy* (Madison, Wisconsin, 1960), p. 155.

[2] Citing, respectively, G. K. Hunter's 'English Folly and Italian Vice', p. 91, and the Introduction to his edition of *Antonio's Revenge*, p. xviii.

The peculiar frisson this may have provided for the play's original audience is hard to recover, but not only is Antonio here putting into practice the most horrifying vengeance Laertes can think of for his father's murderer, 'To cut his throat i'the church' (*Hamlet*, IV.vii.126), but the actor playing the role was himself a choirboy attached to the cathedral of Saint Paul's, and the play was performed in the precincts of the church, so that 'Saint Paul's' echoed underneath 'Saint Mark's'.[1]

The high-flown rhetoric of the large speeches is frequently exposed for the rant that it is by one device or another, from the opening lines when Piero comes on full of 'braggart passion' (I.i.12), and poor Strotzo, urgently trying to convey a message to his master, is interrupted again and again, and allowed only a few phrases and monosyllables, until Piero turns on him to complain:

No! Yes! Nothing but *no* and *yes*, dull lump?
Canst thou not honey me with fluent speech . . . ?

(I.i.83)

The element of comedy in Piero's attack here on the man he has prevented from speaking is sustained throughout. Sometimes it is done by conscious parody, as when Antonio's dream, stuffed with omens and horrors, is absurdly echoed in the fool Balurdo's dream of 'the abominable ghost of a misshapen Simile' (I.ii.103-34). There is frequent recall of earlier styles in the language, with particular echoes of *The Spanish Tragedy* and Seneca; the play contains several reminders that we are watching child-actors strutting like adults; and the players may consciously detach themselves from their roles, as when Alberto and Pandulpho sit down to 'talk as chorus to this tragedy' (I.ii.299), and call for music, which promptly sounds. In addition, the foolish Balurdo is there to comment and deflate throughout, having a part even in the final mask of revengers, and rounding off with an absurd phrase the insults heaped on Piero:

---

[1] The exact location where the Paul's Boys played is not known, but it was 'near St Paules church' (see E. K. Chambers, *The Elizabethan Stage*, II. 22), and may have been within the precincts, possibly in St Gregory's church, which abutted on to the nave of the cathedral.

Antonio	Scum of the mud of hell!
Alberto	Slime of all filth!
Maria	Thou most detested toad!
Balurdo	Thou most retort and obtuse rascal!

(V.iii.96)

The most entertaining example of a conscious use of imitation for comic effect in the play occurs at the opening of Act II, where, after a dumb-show presenting the funeral and coffin of Andrugio, Piero is left to soliloquize in rare passion. Pandulpho has just declared a stoic attitude, refusing to rant in grief for the death of his son Feliche, and saying to Alberto:

> Wouldst have me cry, run raving up and down
> For my son's loss? Wouldst have me turn rank mad,
> Or wring my face with mimic action,
> Stamp, curse, weep, rage, and then my bosom strike?
> Away, 'tis apish action, player-like.

(I.ii.312)

It is just such 'apish action, player-like' an exaggerated tragic rant, that Piero is then given, as he triumphs in the death of his enemy:

> I have but newly twone my arm in the curl'd locks
> Of snaky vengeance. Pale beetle-brow'd hate
> But newly bustles up. Sweet wrong, I clap thy thoughts.
> O, let me hug my bosom, rub my breast,
> In hope of what may hap. Andrugio rots,
> Antonio lives; umh; how long? ha, ha, how long?
> Antonio pack'd hence, I'll his mother wed,
> Then clear my daughter of supposed lust,
> Wed her to Florence heir. O, excellent!
> Venice, Genoa, Florence' at my beck,
> At Piero's nod – Balurdo, O, ho! –
> O, 'twill be rare, all unsuspected done,
> I have been nurs'd in blood, and still have suck'd
> The steam of reeking gore – Balurdo, ho!

(II.i.7)

The melodramatic excess of these lines, which I suspect would raise a laugh in any audience, culminates in the nice reminder that a child is speaking them, as a choirboy is made to cry, 'I have been nurs'd in blood'. At this point he calls for Balurdo, a fool, and a most inappropriate servant for a real villain, who enters, as the stage direction tells us, 'with a beard half off, half on'. He replies to Piero's call,

> When my beard is on, most noble prince, when my
> beard is on.
>
> Piero Why, what dost thou with a beard?
> Balurdo In truth, one told me that my wit was bald, and that
> a mermaid was half fish and half flesh; and therefore
> to speak wisely, like one of your council . . . I must be
> forced to conclude – the tyring man hath not glued on
> my beard half fast enough. God's bores, it will not
> stick to fall off.

This is another echo of *The Spanish Tragedy*; during the preparations for the play that Hieronimo has arranged to grace the betrothal of Balthasar to Bel-Imperia, Balthasar comes on with a property chair, and Hieronimo, as director of his play, urges his actor to make haste:

> Well done, Balthasar! hang up the title:
> Our scene is Rhodes. What, is your beard on?
>
> Balthasar Half on; the other is in my hand.
> Hieronimo Despatch for shame; are you so long?

(IV.iii.16)

Here it is fitting, and quite serious, that Balthasar should be dressing to play Soliman in Hieronimo's production of the play within the play; but Balurdo's entrance interrupts the main action, and the effect is to emphasize the grotesque exaggeration of Piero's language, to detach the characters from their roles, reminding the audience that they are watching actors consciously playing parts, and to generate a special kind of humour out of the clash between Piero's passion and Balurdo's deflating chatter.

The passionate bombast of Antonio:

> Look how I smoke in blood, reeking the steam
> Of foaming vengeance . . . ,

(III.ii.79)

and of Piero:

> Swell plump, bold heart,
> For now thy tide of vengeance rolleth in.
> O now Tragoedia Cothurnata mounts . . . ,

(II.ii.218)

was presented in a parodistic relationship to the language of adult actors in plays like *The Spanish Tragedy*, in which Hieronimo calls for:

> *Tragœdia cothurnata*, fitting kings,
> Containing matter, and not common things.
>
> (IV.i.154)

Pandulpho reminds the audience of this in the curious scene in which he lays the body of Feliche 'thwart Antonio's breast' as Antonio lies prostrate in misery, but disguised as a fool, on the stage; Pandulpho weeps too, and cries:

> Why, all this while I ha' but play'd a part,
> Like to some boy that acts a tragedy,
> Speaks burly words and raves out passion;
> But when he thinks upon his infant weakness,
> He droops his eye. I spake more than a god,
> Yet am less than a man.
>
> (IV.ii.70)

The peculiar tone of the play is in part generated through the exploitation of the clash and incongruity between the 'infant weakness' of the boys, and their 'passion'. They have just been trying to console themselves with arguments borrowed from Seneca's *De Remediis Fortuitorum*, but at this point Antonio 'starts up', throwing off the corpse of Feliche, and they swell into cries for vengeance, going off with their 'arms wreathed'. They speak more than gods, but at the same time, Marston does not let his audience forget that his players are less than men.

The play is designed as a vehicle for child-actors consciously ranting in oversize parts, and we are not allowed to take their passions or motives very seriously. Their grand speeches do not spring from a developed emotional situation, and are undermined by discontinuities, incongruous juxtapositions, and effects of bathos, so that we are not moved by them, but are rather encouraged to maintain a detachment from them. It is a constant aspect of Marston's technique in this play that it simultaneously inflates, in tragic hyperbole, and diminishes, in the figures of child-actors ranting, the stock idea of hero and villain. The many echoes, quotations and repetitions of stage effects from Kyd and Seneca are changed or exaggerated to suggest a mockery of conventional tragic attitudes. So Antonio enters in II.ii with a book of Seneca's philosophical writing in imitation of Hieronimo's entry carrying a volume of Seneca's plays (*The Spanish Tragedy*, III.xiii); Antonio rejects Seneca's preaching of patience in *De Providentia*, preferring to be 'fir'd with impatience', while Hieronimo, rejecting the exhortations of Agamemnon to 'strike home' seeks to subject his 'heart to patience'; but then Antonio ends the scene a 'prostrate wretch' lying full of woe as if 'on his tomb', while Hieronimo goes off in a passion for revenge. Here Antonio merely reverses and exaggerates the change of mood, but such reversals and ex- aggerations can be used to a more potent effect. Perhaps the best example is another echo of *The Spanish Tragedy* in the initial entry of the villain Piero 'his arms bare, smear'd in blood, a poniard in one hand, bloody, and a torch in the other, Strotzo following him with a cord'; this recalls, but with the addition of the blood and the torch, the entry of Hieronimo 'with a poniard in one hand and a rope in the other' (III.xii). Hieronimo is contemplating suicide, Piero congratulating him- self on the murder of Feliche, and Marston has made the effect even more sensational. Not content with one use of it, he goes on to employ it again in III.ii, where this time Antonio comes on stage 'his arms bloody, a torch and a poniard'. This must be intended as a deliberate shock; Piero, the villain, came on rejoicing in the death of Feliche, and now Antonio triumphs in the slaying of the boy Julio. Their deeds are made visually identical, and Marston equates villain and hero here. At the end of the play Piero is cruelly killed after his tongue has been plucked out, and after he has been offered a Thyestean feast of limbs of his dead son by Antonio. As the killers now boast and wrangle about which of them actually murdered Piero, they are greeted, to their amazement, by some senators as saviours, 'Religiously held sacred', and they go off finally to live

> enclos'd
> In holy verge of some religious order,
> Most constant votaries.

(V.iii.151)

The deliberate disregard for moral consistency goes together with another reminder that the actors are choirboys playing in the 'holy verge' of Saint Paul's. This last scene can only be interpreted as consciously outrageous, flouting with calculated enormity a conventional ending which would have punished Antonio.

If a serious purpose is to be found here, it is best defined in terms of an interest in 'the cold realities of power',[1] the rejection or distortion of accepted values, so that the heroic certainties, the clear oppositions underlying plays like *The Spanish Tragedy* or *Hamlet*, are made to look old-fashioned. However, the main impact of the play is melodramatic and satirical, and the satire is directed less against folly and vice than against conventional literary and theatrical styles, attitudes and moral patterns. Because of this it was an achievement of a sort that could not be repeated, though its innovations of technique and attitude made a significant impact on later plays. At some time between 1600 and 1604, when *The Malcontent* was published, the new style of Marston was heard on the stage of the Globe theatre. For their performance of the play, Shakespeare's company provided additions to take the place of the interludes of music customary in the children's theatres. The additions written by John Webster include an Induction in which one actor, Sinklo, bets that 'the play is not so well acted as it hath been', and a number of passages which expand the comic dialogue in the play by adding a fool, Passarello, and elaborating the part of the old corrupt courtier, Bilioso. The additions also provided more for Burbage, who played Malevole, to speak, chiefly in exchanges with Passarello and Bilioso, but also by enlarging one or two of his big speeches in the opening and closing scenes. Both the Induction, which self-consciously calls attention to the artifice of the play, and the other additions expanding the foolery in the action, seem designed to reinforce the comic, even absurd mood which the children could establish naturally by aping adult-actors.

If these elements, like Marston's address to the reader, and the prologue, all emphasize that the play is a comedy, and the

---

[1] Citing Hunter, 'English Folly and Italian Vice', p. 91. It would be less than fair to Hunter not to note how far he differs from me in his account of *Antonio's Revenge*, as he developed this in his edition (1965), pp. xiii-xiv, where he argues that Marston, as a serious student of Seneca, had an 'obsession with violence and evil, seen as pressing everywhere on the life even of the good man', and that the play offers a 'coherent and concentrated expression of the human alternatives in the Christian-Stoic ethical vision'.

author's pen 'still must write of fools, whiles't writes of men' (Prologue, l. 14), nevertheless, it seems, like *Antonio's Revenge*, to point the way to a self-conscious, satirical mode of tragedy, rather than to developments in comedy. The idea of the Duke in disguise watching over the corruptions in his state links the play with *Measure for Measure*, but this is not an important connection. It may be more properly seen as looking forward to *The Revenger's Tragedy*, but it is important to notice its limitations in this respect. After the brilliant outrageousness of the *Antonio* plays Marston seems steadily to have drawn in his horns. *The Malcontent* is in some ways an advance. Malevole nicely draws into one role Antonio and Balurdo, combining something of the grandiose heroic stance of the one, with the grotesque foolery of the other; it may be that Burbage made something of this character, passionate, melancholy, stoic and absurd by turns, but the play is clearly designed to prevent us from taking him or it too seriously. The main interest is in intrigue; the insistence on the externality of the action, the intricate arrangements of effects, as in the use of multiple disguises, the conscious staging, and the exaggerations of the language all establish a tonality that undermines Malevole's attacks on court-corruption and his enthusiasm for 'fearless virtue' (I.iv.13).

It seems to me doubtful whether this play really evokes a 'profound sense of moral distress', or provides a 'successful fusion of the solemn and grotesque', as has been claimed for it.[1] The ingenuity of the action always seems more interesting than its moral nature. Malevole, the disguised Duke of Genoa, claims to be an Asper playing the role of Macilente:

> Hope, hope, that never forsak'st the wretched'st man,
> Yet bidd'st me live and lurk in this disguise!
> What, play I well the free-breath'd discontent?
> Why, man, we are all philosophical monarchs
> Or natural fools. Celso, the court's afire;
> The duchess' sheets will smoke for't ere it be long.
> Impure Mendoza, that sharp-nos'd lord, that made
> The cursed match link'd Genoa with Florence,

[1] The phrases are from Antony Caputi's *John Marston, Satirist* (1961), pp. 196 and 198.

Now broad-horns the duke, which he now knows.
Discord to malcontents is very manna;
When the ranks are burst, then scuffle, Altofront.

(I.iv.29)

Something serious could have been made of the clash between his claim to be a 'philosophical monarch' superior to the folly of others, and his enjoyment of lust in others, his delight in discord. In fact the two stances remain separate, and the second one provides the prevailing note of the play. In this Malevole is seconded by Mendoza, who is also contriving discord in the court usurped by Pietro. So now when Malevole informs Pietro that he is being cuckolded by Mendoza, he does not know that Ferneze has replaced Mendoza in the affections of Aurelia. Marston is thus able to create two fine melodramatic scenes, one in which Mendoza is confronted by Pietro with drawn sword, and jests his way out of death to persuade Pietro that Ferneze is the man:

	Enter Pietro, *his sword drawn.*
Pietro	A mischief fill thy throat, thou foul-jaw'd slave.
	Say thy prayers.
Mendoza	I ha' forgot 'em.
Pietro	Thou shalt die!
Mendoza	So shalt thou. I am heart-mad.
Pietro	I am horn-mad.
Mendoza	Extreme mad.
Pietro	Monstrously mad.
Mendoza	Why?
Pietro	Why? Thou, thou hast dishonoured my bed.

(I.vii.1)

Whether Mendoza's replies here be taken as impudent, or mocking, or careless, they effectively empty the situation of danger and expose Pietro's stance as ineffective; if Mendoza were in immediate danger of death, he would not reply so wittily to 'Thou shalt die' with a reminder that all men must eventually, 'So shalt thou'.

The other scene is that in which Ferneze comes out of Aurelia's bedroom to be 'received' on the sword of Mendoza (II.v), and drops 'dead' before Aurelia on the stage. Mendoza stays to convince Aurelia that Pietro is to blame for this, and they conspire together to murder Pietro 'Instantly' (l. 74).

Mendoza then employs Malevole to bury the body of Ferneze, but as soon as Malevole is left alone on stage, Ferneze, who has been lying there 'dead' for 140 lines, comes to life, and turns out to be merely wounded after all. This provides an occasion for Malevole to preach against lust:

> But fame ne'er heals, still rankles worse and worse;
> Such is of uncontrolled lust the curse.
> Think what it is in lawless sheets to lie;
> But, O, Ferneze, what in lust to die!

(II.v.146)

The sermon bears little relation to the action. Ferneze's offence is to have slept with Aurelia, who already commits adultery with Mendoza, and whose virtue is as easy as that of Maquerelle and her ladies of the court; 'fame' in this court appears to lie in the number of conquests a man or woman can make rather than in a chaste life. This is no rape, and cannot be taken seriously as adultery, and Ferneze shows no concern for his fame; while for all their talk of murder neither Mendoza nor Pietro can ever manage to carry one out. The moral implications of each situation tend to evaporate, and we are left with fine theatrical moments and entertaining, sometimes absurd, intrigues.

These reach a climax when in IV.iv Malevole and Pietro, now disguised as a hermit, confront one another, and discover they have each been hired by Mendoza to kill the other by the same means and at the same time:

Malevole How do you? How dost, duke?

Pietro O, let the last day fall! Drop, drop on our cursed heads! Let heaven unclasp itself, vomit forth flames.

Malevole O, do not rant, do not turn player. There's more of them than can well live one by another already. What, art an infidel still?

Pietro I am amaz'd, struck in a swoon with wonder. I am commanded to poison thee.

Malevole I am commanded to poison thee at supper.

Pietro At supper?

Malevole In the citadel.

Pietro In the citadel?

Malevole Cross-capers! Tricks!

(IV.iv.1)

The effect of this is surely intended to be comic, to draw attention to the 'cross-capers', as Malevole stops Pietro from ranting with a gratuitous joke about actors in London; at the same time, by exposing Pietro's outcry as bombast, Malevole is also discouraging the audience from taking him seriously when he 'turns player' a little later in the scene to declaim:

> World: 'Tis the only region of death, the greatest shop of the devil, the cruel'st prison of men, out of the which none pass without paying their dearest breath for a fee . . . .
>
> (IV.iv.27)

Indeed, such pronouncements, expressions of Malevole's melancholy and moral indignation, are to a large extent subverted by the nature of the play, its comic tone, its tendency to relax and play with situations, to exploit intrigue and melodrama for their own sakes, to be too conscious of itself; no one suffers much because in the context no one sins much in a world where no one thinks twice about lust or murder, and where much is intended, but little in fact happens. Malevole's perfunctory moral comment at the end (expanded by Webster), and his quick dispensation of rewards and punishments, count for little except as a winding up of the action. One wonders what he will now do for entertainment in Genoa, and his wife Maria, at last released after a long, chaste and dull imprisonment, seems merely to have missed all the fun.

At the same time, this play comes nearer than *Antonio's Revenge* to realizing serious potentialities for satirical tragedy. Malevole as master-intriguer posing as fool-villain and enjoying his satirical superiority over the rest of the court, sorts uneasily with the lofty, noble and upright Altofronto, Duke of Genoa. There is no convincing connection between the two, and their identity is exploited for neat theatrical effects, as in the masque at the end, where Malevole and his companions surround the villain Mendoza with pistols aimed at him, and 'unmask', revealing Altofronto and Pietro. Mendoza expects death, but is granted life, and Marston gives a new twist to the masque at the end, which had brought death to the villains in both *The Spanish Tragedy* and *Antonio's Revenge*. The logic of Malevole's character, all the same, might lead us to expect him to fall in love with the role he so much enjoys playing, that of intriguer, but it was left to the author of *The Revenger's Tragedy* to develop this idea and so create one of the masterpieces of the drama of this period. Malevole never has to struggle to keep separate the two roles he is playing, and can always drop his disguise and appear as Altofronto with no difficulty; this is only possible because the rather self-conscious comedy of the play never permits any real villainy to be carried through. By contrast, Vindice in *The Revenger's Tragedy* is contaminated from the start by the sins he condemns in others, and his powerful denunciations of the evil in the court show his growing involvement in the viciousness he attacks.

Vindice makes himself the master-intriguer in a court devoted to plot and counter-plot. Like Malevole, he acts as a commentator on the action, in his disguise as malcontent or bawd, and from his cry 'be merry' in his opening speech, he clowns, exercises his wit in tricks and quibbles, and guides our appreciation of what happens by his satiric comments. Unlike Malevole, however, he comes to delight in his own artistry so much that he loses sight of the horror of what he is himself doing, as when he gloats over the means he has found of poisoning the Duke, by having him kiss the anointed skull of the dead Gloriana, and cries:

O sweet, delectable, rare, happy, ravishing!

(III.v.1)

What the play shows as the action progresses is the growing distance between this aspect of Vindice, lost 'in a throng of happy apprehensions' (III.v.30) as he relishes the thought of murder, and that other perspective in which Vindice likes to see himself, as Heaven's instrument, sent

To blast this villainous dukedom, vex'd with sin.

(V.ii.6)

It is fitting that at the end Vindice should be so carried away by his success in intrigue that he forgets his moral stance altogether for a moment, and so reveals publicly what he now is, acknowledging that he and Hippolito contrived the death of the old Duke:

'twas somewhat witty caried, though we say it. 'Twas we two murdered him.

F

(V.iii.97-8)

Although we are continually reminded of the ironic distance between what Vindice preaches and what he practises, he nevertheless is so much the stage-manager of the complicated intrigues of the action that our view of it is in large measure guided by him; that he sees the action as macabre, grotesque, and often funny, helps to shape our view of events, and to ensure that we do not mistake what we see for an illusion of reality. His perspective ensures that we view the characters and their fantastic intrigues with a satirical detachment; the naming of the characters as embodiments of lust (Lussurioso), ambition (Ambitioso), and other vices or virtues is matched by the treatment of them as comic-grotesque figures, emblematic moral examples, distanced from us also by their constant use of proverbs, maxims and couplets. Their moral capacity is limited to sententious phrases that prove to be grossly inadequate, absurdly misapplied, or relevant with an irony they do not understand; and their attitudes shift constantly as they are remade for each situation. The generalizing force of their comments suggests a concern for morality and truth which is quite unrelated to their behaviour, and is never tested against principles. It is a mechanical sententiousness they possess, comically horrible; the Duke, Lussurioso, and all the courtiers are experts in the manipulation of such utterances, which punctuate their speech in lines like these:

> I know this, which I never learn'd in schools:
> The world's divided into knaves and fools.
>
> (II.ii.4-5)

>   this true reason gathers:
> None can possess that dispossess their fathers.
>
> (II.iii.85-6)

> The falling of one head lifts up another.
>
> (III.i.28)

> Slaves are but nails, to drive out one another.
>
> (IV.i.68)

The neatness of a couplet, or the support of some proverb expanded into a sententious utterance, may lend an appearance of justification to vicious inclinations, and an aura of time-honoured wisdom to the nasty satisfactions of revenge. Since all the characters except Vindice and Hippolito his brother are black or white, devoted to evil or good (Castiza), and Gratiana is the only one who changes, being forced to repent her viciousness at the point of a dagger, the effect is to distance them within a framework of moral comment which continually exposes the grotesque nature of what they are about.

Vindice alone in the unspecified Italian court of the play recognizes the possibility of a sane balance and, with his sister Castiza, of a healthy morality; after meditating in his most famous speech on the way in which everyone devoted his energies to the pursuit of a 'bewitching minute', the momentary gratification of lust, Vindice cries:

> Surely we are all mad people, and they
> Whom we think are, are not; we mistake those:
> 'Tis we are mad in sense, they but in clothes.
>
> (III.v.80-2)

He appropriately includes himself, as caught up in the madness of intrigue, and his words also embrace the audience, so involving us in the momentary shock of recognizing ourselves as potentially there. But our fuller sense of the world of the play as one in which the characters are in some sense 'mad' and distanced from us remains the controlling perspective. The play has great concentration and intensity, and never relaxes, as Marston's plays do, to jest with the audience and exploit a conscious theatricality; Vindice's savage humour, and his passionate devotion to revenge are kept in balance, so that those comments of his that include the audience in their scope suggest for a moment that for some of us life is, and for all could be, no more than such an interlude of lust, treachery, revenge, and murder, as the play shows:

> If every trick were told that's dealt by night,
> There are few here that would not blush outright.
>
> (II.ii.148-9)

>   see, ladies, with false forms
> You deceive men, but cannot deceive worms.
>
> (III.v.97-8)

As a whole the play does not touch us so nearly, but demands to be taken emblematically, as a type of what a human society might be at its worst, all its bestial passions released, and all its store of proverbial wisdom and moral sententiae made ineffective because unrelated to deeply felt emotions or strongly held principles. Here satire and tragedy come together, taking us, as it were, to the edge of a precipice, and showing us, in the gulf beyond, a limiting possibility of a society where social, legal and moral restraints have crumbled away. The play provides a fearful lesson or moral image, but its limitations as tragedy need to be noted too. The characters are mostly types, capable of making moral glosses on their actions, but lacking self-realization; they are aspects of a monstrous fantasy, which powerfully succeeds in making its point, but the price paid for its success is a loss of the common touch, of that representative quality which allows heroic tragedy to speak for everyman.[1]

Perhaps the most interesting attempt to bridge satire and tragedy was Ben Jonson's in *Sejanus*, acted, as the 1616 Folio tells us, by the King's Men in 1603, with Shakespeare as one of the actors. The play failed on its first performance, was published in 1605, and at some time between then and 1616, was revived successfully on the stage. The reasons for the play's initial failure are not to be found in Jonson's concern for his classical sources, which were noted in the margin of the Quarto, but rather in the revolutionary nature of the play. For here, as in *Everyman Out of his Humour*, Jonson seems to have been very much an innovator. For this strong and often brilliantly written play pursues the logic of its theme to a savage conclusion, and must have seemed very strange to an audience accustomed to heroic tragedy of the kind represented by *Hamlet*. Sejanus, the monstrous opportunist at the centre of the action, uses murder and political intrigue to make himself the most powerful man in Rome, even dominating, as he thinks, the emperor Tiberius. In fact Tiberius, alert to possible danger, outmanœuvres Sejanus by employing Macro to spy on him, even though he knows there is 'none less apt for trust' (III.650).

---

[1] Some of the argument here is taken from the Introduction to my edition of *The Revenger's Tragedy* (Revels Plays, 1966), pp. xix-xlv.

Macro might be speaking for Tiberius, and Sejanus, as well as himself when he rejoices in being employed by Tiberius:

> Were it to plot against the fame, the life
> Of one with whom I twinn'd; remove a wife
> From my warm side, as lov'd, as is the air;
> Practise away each parent; draw mine heir
> In compass, though but one; work all my kin
> To swift perdition; leave no untrain'd engine,
> For friendship, or for innocence; nay, make
> The gods all guilty: I would undertake
> This, being impos'd me, both with gain, and ease.
> The way to rise, is to obey, and please.
>
> (III.726)

In this readiness to do anything, and betray his 'friend' Sejanus for his own advancement, Macro proposes quite seriously to follow a course of wholly unscrupulous evil, such as is made tolerable in *The Revenger's Tragedy* only through the comic horror and satiric exaggerations of Vindice's perspective on events. Here there is little or nothing to choose between Sejanus, Macro, who in the end supplants him and will prove to be just like him, or the corrupt Tiberius, who is content to rule through such ministers.

The good characters in the play, notably Sabinus, Silius and Arruntius, act as Aspers, commenting on the vices they see around them, sharply and satirically aware of the true nature of Sejanus and the emperor; but because they refuse to adopt the weapons of the corrupt, they remain powerless. The only stance available to them is a stoic one, claiming a superiority over Fortune while waiting in hope that her wheel will turn, or the gods intervene, to destroy the evils afflicting Rome. They may gain some satisfaction in seeing the hated Sejanus fall as he over-reaches himself in aiming to marry into royal blood, and crow a little, like Arruntius and Lepidus:

> *Arruntius* Who would trust slippery chance?
> *Lepidus*   They, that would make
> Themselves her spoil: and foolishly forget,
> When she doth flatter, that she comes to prey.
> Fortune, thou hadst no deity, if men

> Had wisdom: we have placed thee so high,
> By fond belief in thy felicity.
>
> (V.733)

However, their role is limited to such minor triumphs, as they watch what happens, and wait their own turn to bleed when the emperor or his ministers find them too much of a nuisance. Then their best moment may come, as it does for Silius, impeached by device before the Senate in Act III. Rejecting the accusations made against him as the plots of Sejanus, he 'mocks' the tyranny of Tiberius, and shows himself superior to Fortune, by stabbing himself; suicide becomes an heroic act, and the only way in the end to retain self-respect and the respect of others when, as Sabinus says:

> A good man should and must
> Sit rather down with loss, than rise unjust
>
> (IV.165)

At the same time, their appeals to the gods to intervene and overthrow the vice of 'these impious times' go unanswered; Arruntius cries, 'Jove, will nothing wake thee?' (IV.266), and at last the gods, or Fortune, seem to take a hand, as Macro and Tiberius conspire to bring about the downfall of Sejanus, and Terentius moralizes:

> Let this example move th'insolent man,
> Not to grow proud, and careless of the gods.
>
> (V.898)

His words are undercut, however, by several kinds of irony. In the first place, as Arruntius realizes, Macro will prove to be another Sejanus. Secondly, the 'rude multitude' so savagely tear Sejanus to pieces, and murder his innocent children, that, 'transported with their cruelty' (V.817), they seem to embody at large the very evils for which they destroy Sejanus. Thirdly, Arruntius, Lepidus and the other Asper-like commentators on the action, who represent the opposition to tyranny, belong to the circle of the virtuous Agrippina, and we recognize that if their prayers for an end to the tyranny of Tiberius were to be answered, the succession would go to Caligula, who would prove to be just as bad. It is a savage world, in which nothing redeems the viciousness of the central figures, and the good are limited to expressing their feelings in their moralizing or satirical commentary. Jonson's tactic is to make us see the main action through the eyes of these commentators, and so to maintain a detachment from the central characters; and we are not involved in the fall of Sejanus so much as in the tragic condition of Rome, exemplified at the end in the behaviour of a mob that is as cruel as its hated masters. The world of the play is a dark and cruel one, in which the good are shown as impotent; it anticipates in some ways the 'gloomy world' of Webster's plays, and the assumption of corruption as the norm in Middleton's tragedies. It must have seemed very strange at the Globe in 1603, and it is not surprising that an audience attuned to *Hamlet*, or even *The Malcontent*, should have reacted violently against it.

(ii) SHAKESPEARE, FROM *Hamlet* TO *Coriolanus*

These three plays, *The Malcontent*, *Sejanus* and *The Revenger's Tragedy*, were all performed by Shakespeare's company between 1603 and 1606, and brought home on the stage of the Globe theatre the potentialities for a new kind of tragedy developed by Marston and Jonson in particular. Each exploits a satirical distancing of its action in a different way; *The Malcontent* seems in the end to be self-consciously playing with theatrical effects; *Sejanus* offers a bleak vision of a world wholly given over to intrigue and murder for political ends, but distanced and so made endurable through the satirical perspective provided by a group of commentators; *The Revenger's Tragedy* integrates the witty detachment that becomes an end in itself in Marston's plays into a new mode of satirical tragedy, in which the protagonist's satirical stance is made to take effect fully as a part of the play's serious action. During these same years, Shakespeare was clearly influenced by the new comedy of the children's stages in writing the 'dark' comedies, but seems to have absorbed more cautiously the spirit of the new tragedy. He continued in the four central tragedies of this period, *Hamlet*, *Othello*, *King Lear* and *Macbeth*, to write plays which take themselves seriously as heroic tragedies, and which demand from us a full engagement with the hero.

The Malcontent and *The Revenger's Tragedy* both have links with *Hamlet*, which, in the text represented by the good Quarto of 1604, shows Shakespeare's awareness of the new success of the children's companies after 1600. This is apparent not only in the conversation between Hamlet and Rosencrantz reporting that the boy-players are all the rage, 'cry out on top of the question, and are most tyrannically clapped for't' (II.ii.336), but also in the development of satirical stances in Hamlet himself. At the same time, the satirical elements in the play, like the concern with the playing of roles, and the contrast between old and new styles of acting suggested by the play within the play, are all contained within the action, and are not used as a means of distancing it. This may be illustrated by a brief consideration of one tactic common to these plays, the use of images of or references to the theatre within the action. Frequently in *Antonio's Revenge*, and occasionally in *The Malcontent*, Marston disengages his characters momentarily from their roles to make them comment directly on the action, the actors, or audience, as when Pandulfo and Alberto decide to sit and 'talk as chorus to this tragedy', or when Malevole stops Pietro in his rant by saying, 'do not turn player; there's more of them than can well live one by another already'. It is one of the tactics Marston uses to distance the action and prevent us from a full emotional engagement with it. In *The Revenger's Tragedy*, there are a number of references to or images of the theatre, but they are used not to detach characters from the roles, rather to take effect within the serious action of the play, while at the same time being open to interpretation as comments on that action; in other words, they are absorbed into and held in control by the main action. So when Vindice uses the skull of his dead mistress to poison the Duke, he sees himself as staging a revenge play of his own:

> Now to my tragic business, look you brother,
> I have not fashioned this only for show
> And useless property; no, it shall bear a part
> E'en in its own revenge.

(III.v.100)

This scene has links with *Hamlet*, in which the hero plays many roles, and fancies himself as an actor with the company of travelling players that comes to Elsinore. There is yet another, and important, difference here, however, in that Hamlet is wholly, emotionally and morally, involved in making his decision, questioning his own purposes, whereas Vindice has made his decision before the play opens, and announces it in his first speech. Vindice's attention is thus focused on the question, how to effect his revenge in the neatest way, and because he is concerned only with the means, he becomes caught up in his own cleverness, and in the delight of stage-managing his own little play in which he murders the Duke. Hamlet, by contrast, is occupied with the end, and hence with the moral and emotional dilemma in which he is placed. In spite of the elements of satire in *Hamlet*, and the awareness of the theatre shown in it, extending to the topical allusion to the success of the children's companies, it remains basically an heroic tragedy, which depends for its effect on our full engagement with the hero.

Hamlet, indeed, is powerfully presented as a representative of a world of Christian ethics and heroic ideals. It is an idea mirrored for him in the vision he retains of his father, the image he sees, or thinks he sees, in the armed ghost, and which is figured in Horatio's report of the old Hamlet as one who was challenged by old Fortinbras to single combat, and undertook the fight in chivalric manner, as 'ratified by law and heraldry'. Hamlet retains a somewhat naïve and idealistic image of his father:

Hyperion's curls, the front of Jove himself,
An eye like Mars, to threaten and command,

(III.iv.56)

this godlike image, however inappropriate to the ghost crying revenge, embodies for him the idea of an heroic world in which he, as a man of principle, could move freely. But he finds himself in a world of craft and double-dealing in the court of Denmark; where old Hamlet could settle matters according to the laws of chivalry, in single combat, Claudius deals with Norway by diplomacy.

In his clash with Claudius, representative of a world of politics and assays of bias, Hamlet seems to clutch more and more at the idea of providence until, when he stabs Polonius, he cries:

> Heaven hath pleas'd it so
> To punish me with this and this with me
> That I must be their scourge and minister.

(III.iv.173)

In this kind of appeal or claim, Hamlet accommodates himself
to the idea of murder and the sacrifice of his principles, by
interpreting what he is doing as the will of heaven, and so saves
his self-respect:

> is't not perfect conscience
> To quit him with this arm? And is't not to be damn'd
> To let this canker of our nature come
> In further evil?

(V.ii.67)

Here Hamlet sees himself as judge and executioner, but Heaven
has not appointed him to 'quit' or revenge himself on Claudius;
he was right when he said of the death of Polonius, 'This bad
begins, and worse remains behind' (III.iv.179). The Christian
colouring of the play does not make it a specifically Christian
tragedy; the tragic effect springs rather from the human
dilemma registered in the clash of ethics and politics. What we
can say is that the world Hamlet would belong to is the Christian
humanist world in which the heroic ideal fosters and enlarges
the Christian idea of a good man; and that the assumption of
this world that man can elevate himself to enjoy his own divine
essence is rudely shattered in conflict with the world of Claudius,
where moral certainties are destroyed. It is often said that Hamlet
is an image of modernity in his scepticism, his uncertainty about
values in the Denmark ruled by Claudius; but I think the sense
of modernity in the play arises rather out of the clash between
two worlds. If anything, Claudius is the more modern figure,
and Hamlet is almost old-fashioned as the moral man, the
Christian man of principle.

The satirical distancing and mockery of the heroic protagonist shown in plays of Marston at this time, and the absorption
of satire more fully into tragedy by Ben Jonson and Tourneur,
or whoever wrote *The Revenger's Tragedy*, suggest indeed that
Hamlet was a little old-fashioned even when it was written.
Hamlet the prince was turned into a footman, servant to a
foolish Gertrude, in *Eastward Ho!* (1605), and this mockery

in a children's play perhaps reflects the shift that was taking place at the time. Hamlet is one of the last great representatives of a dying mode, heroic tragedy, and part of our perpetual interest in him springs from our nostalgia for the world of certainties he represents; the play shows him forced by the pressure of events to adapt his ideals to the world of politics, and in this sense it may be read almost as an allegory of the history of our civilization. At the same time, the politic reach and wisdom of Claudius is shown as corrupt, and the moral opposition between him and Hamlet is basically the clear conflict of evil versus good, even if in the end Hamlet is driven to corrupt himself by using the tactics of Claudius to bring about his revenge.

Whatever their differences, and allowing for the degree to which *King Lear* especially raises difficulties and escapes simple categories, it remains true, as many have observed, that the four central tragedies all deal basically with a clash of good and evil, and require of us a commitment to the good. They are all heroic tragedies, in which the clash of fell and mighty opposites represents a conflict of absolute values, as evil brings chaos to the potentially good man, Othello, or lays waste the kingdoms of Lear or Macbeth, temporarily disturbing or overthrowing an order that is potentially good. *Hamlet* is particularly interesting for my argument because it presents this opposition to a large extent in the clash of old and new, old ethics and new politics, and because it was so closely connected with, and partly provoked, the innovations of Marston and Tourneur (if he wrote *The Revenger's Tragedy*). Shakespeare came to exploit the new possibilities for tragedy opened up by these and Ben Jonson only in his later tragedies, those written after *Macbeth*. In *Timon of Athens*, *Coriolanus* and *Antony and Cleopatra*, the terms of the conflict are changed, as the central figures are not shown as clashing with or trapped by evil, but rather as unable to adapt themselves to a world of relative values which sanctions the flexible man (like Alcibiades) in place of the man of absolutes (like Timon). These plays have no villains, and in them the abilities of Claudius (leaving aside the murder of the old Hamlet) count for more than the moral virtue of Hamlet.

This may be seen in the new tragic pairings to be found in the later plays, beginning with Timon and Alcibiades. Timon's very virtues become in a sense his vices; his generosity will not allow others to be bountiful to him, and he acts as though Plutus the god of gold were his steward:

> 'Tis not enough to give;
> Methinks I could deal kingdoms to my friends,
> And ne'er be weary.

> (I.ii.219)

Other men do not exist for him except as objects of his bounty, or projections of himself, and in his self-love he forbids others to give, or even to repay. His bountiful nobility is perverted by a refined selfishness, which blinds him to the practices of others; in a way he forces his 'friends' to treat him as a fool, who, properly flattered, makes his flatterers rich. As they have used him for a gold-mine, so they cast him off when his wealth is gone, and the self-centred generosity of the rich Timon is transformed inevitably into its obverse, a self-centred misanthropy. Timon is here the man of absolutes; completely noble, generous and free, he yet shows that bounty mars men, who may not act like gods. In his self-imposed exile from Athens he encourages Alcibiades the warrior to descend like a plague on the 'high-vic'd city' of Athens, ruled by the senators who grew rich on Timon's gifts. But although Alcibiades stood apart from the other guests at Timon's feasts as one who was not concerned to grow rich, he does not appear as a great deliverer at the end. This is no champion of good against evil, no golden boy, like Malcolm cleansing Scotland, or Edgar returning as a knight in shining armour to joust with and defeat the evil embodied in Edmund, but the general Alcibiades, who carries prostitutes in his train, defends murderers, and is content with 'defil'd land' as his home. He is merely the soldier, doing what he conceives to be his duty, and acting for private reasons as much as for public welfare, as he goes to Athens partly to carry out a private revenge:

> Soldiers should brook as little wrongs as gods.

> (III.v.118)

The hero as potentially an ideal figure, involved in a struggle against evil, vanishes here in Timon's 'wretched corse, of wretched soul bereft', and there is something like a reversal of the roles of Hamlet and Claudius as Alcibiades, the adaptable man, *l'homme moyen sensuel*, the descendant of Claudius, takes over and brings order, peace, and a rough justice to Athens. To call this a 'reversal' of roles is, of course, an exaggeration, but it is a useful exaggeration if it draws attention to important differences. Timon's special virtue, generosity, becomes a fault, and the clear moral distinctions of the central tragedies become blurred; the difference between love and lust is clear in *Hamlet*, but not in *Antony and Cleopatra*, where it is impossible to draw a line between the magnificence of Antony's passion and the corrupting effect of his lust; and the virtues of Coriolanus prove to be destructive. The flexible man, the more skilful politician, survives in the world of these plays – Alcibiades, Octavius, Aufidius. The protagonists are presented critically, and distanced from us in the discordances of a variety of perspectives upon them. One of these perspectives is provided by a satirical spokesman who is relatively independent of the main action, however much he may be a friend of the hero, like Menenius or Enobarbus – these are not cynic railers like Apemantus, a true descendant of Macilente, but they know the faults of Coriolanus and Antony. It is in these plays that Shakespeare adapts to his own purposes the possibilities for satirical tragedy opened up by Marston and Jonson.

Coriolanus perhaps points up the contrasts with *Hamlet* most clearly. In *Hamlet*, as I have argued earlier, the hero, as a man of principle living in the light of the chivalric ideals for which his father seemed to stand, clashes with the politic Claudius, whose world is shown as corrupt; and in the end, although Hamlet has to involve himself in the corrupt ways of Claudius to effect his revenge, it is in order to cleanse the court of Denmark and rid it of evil. Hamlet gives his dying vote to Fortinbras, a 'delicate and tender Prince', who revives the image of warrior King shattered in the death of old King Hamlet, and will renew the heroic ideal of Elsinore. In the conflict here of the old chivalric code and the new art of politics, the old values are sanctioned, and we give our sympathy wholly to Hamlet. In *Coriolanus* Shakespeare also portrayed the clash of old and new values, but with a difference. The Rome of this play is in the process of becoming more democratic as drastic political changes are being forced upon it. At the start of the play, the people have won the right to choose five tribunes to represent them, and the two we meet in the play, Brutus and Sicinius, are middle-class, educated figures, men of some wealth, as Brutus himself indicates when he wishes half his wealth would buy the news of the return of Coriolanus to Rome for a lie (IV.iv.160). They are politicians who lead the mob with words, just as Coriolanus leads his army with actions. The old Menenius, once a soldier, and the lover of Marcius, has turned politician, and, left to himself, could more than match the tribunes and the people, as he shows in calming the mob with his fable of the belly in the opening scene. He mocks the tribunes, and encourages them to think of him as 'a perfecter giber for the table than a necessary bencher in the Capitol' (II.i.76), but Brutus is accepting too readily Menenius' own version of himself as a 'humorous patrician'.

Menenius has adapted himself to the new political order, in which the patricians and the people might negotiate in words, and civility prevail; he might be seen as a representative of urbanity. So, in her way, is Virgilia, who, when we first see her, cannot bear the thought of her husband Marcius at the wars, and who stands weeping and silent when he returns in triumph as Coriolanus in II.i; here she embodies eloquently enough those qualities he holds of no account or does not comprehend, pity, tenderness, humility, the common affections. Her tears express her relief that he comes back alive, but represent also the grief of all those new widows whose husbands have come 'coffin'd home', and who, like her, live for peace, not war. As against these, Coriolanus himself appears as the relic of a more barbarous time, when martial virtue was all-important. Shakespeare is much more subtle than Plutarch in presenting his central figure, but developed North's description of Marcius:[1]

> For this Martius' natural wit and great heart did marvelously stir up his courage, to do and attempt notable acts. But on the other side, for lack of education he was so choleric and impatient that he would yield to no living creature, which made him churlish, uncivil, and altogether unfit for any man's conversation.

[1] Cited from *Shakespeare's Plutarch*, edited by T. J. B. Spencer (1964), p. 297.

In the play the incivility of Marcius is shown often enough, and not only in his treatment of the people, whom he speaks of as animals, fragments, or things, but also in his behaviour to the senate, when he refuses to listen to the customary encomium in his praise. In this scene (II.ii) Cominius, praising Coriolanus, gives a brief biography of him, and reports how, as a boy of sixteen, he fought against Tarquin, the last of the kings of Rome:

> At sixteen years,
> When Tarquin made a head for Rome, he fought
> Beyond the mark of others. Our then Dictator,
> Whom with all praise I point at, saw him fight
> When with his Amazonian chin he drove
> The bristled lips before him. He bestrid
> An o'erpress'd Roman, and i' the Consul's view,
> Slew three opposers.

(II.ii.85)

Then martial prowess was valuable, and indeed, as Cominius says, the 'highest virtue', in driving tyranny from Rome, but history has made it less important, useful in keeping the Volscians in order, but no longer the most necessary virtue in Rome itself. It is ironical that Marcius began his career by fighting tyranny, and so helped to initiate the process of change that has led from tyrant, through 'dictator' (does Cominius point to some old senator here? – but not to Menenius, certainly) and 'consul' to the new establishment of tribunes.[1]

Rather than showing the incivility of Marcius as resulting from a lack of education, Shakespeare presents it as the product of the only education he had, at the hands of his mother, who is now complacently enjoying the prospect that the little son of Marcius will be like his father, and 'rather see the swords and hear a drum than look upon his schoolmaster' (I.iii.54). She is delighted to hear Valeria's tale of the boy tearing a butterfly to pieces, as it reflects 'One on's father's moods' (I.iii.66). Volumnia has taught to despise the populace,

> To call them woollen vassals, things created
> To buy and sell with groats, to show bare heads

---

[1] The allusion to the 'dictator' comes from Plutarch: 'Martius valiantly fought in the sight of the Dictator' (*Shakespeare's Plutarch*, p. 298); but Shakespeare added 'Whom with all praise I point at'. Plutarch does not give the name of the dictator.

In congregations, to yawn, be still and wonder
When one but of my ordinance stood up
To speak of peace or war.

(III.ii.9)

She has trained him in the arrogant attitudes of patrician dictatorship, and it is the limitation of his nature that he cannot change, but must 'play The man I am'. After his triumph at Corioli, it is natural for his party, the patricians, to propose him for consul, and to assume that he need do little to carry the election; there is a modern parallel for it in the election of General Eisenhower as President of the United States. But to lead men in battle (where they do not always follow him) is not the same as to rule men in peace. Coriolanus cannot adjust to rule others or himself, however good a leader he may be, and in some measure he knows this; he recognizes that as he prepares to go to the market-place to show himself in the gown of humility:

You have put me now to such a part which never
I shall discharge to the life.

(III.ii.105)

He cannot sustain any other role than what he is, and his noble nature is marred by the psychological limitation of his inflexibility. He can only be a military leader or dictator, and if Rome has no place for him as such (he would have been impossible as Consul), then he is ready to offer his services to Antium, so at once fulfilling the tribunes' accusation that he is a 'traitor'. His allegiance to his idea of himself is more important than his loyalty to his country.

At the end, arrogantly taking over the effective leadership of the Volscians, he besieges Rome, and only the appearance before him of his family makes him forget 'his part' of implacable hostility, and recognize that he cannot finally

stand

As if a man were author of himself,
And knew no other kin.

(V.iii.35)

His mother kneels to him now, recalling his kneeling before Volumnia after his triumphant return from Corioli, and 'this unnatural scene' brings home to him that to be himself he must acknowledge his kin. For his image of himself has always been validated in the mirror of his mother's applause; to destroy Rome would be to shatter that mirror, and to destroy a part of himself. To withdraw, on the other hand, is almost certainly to destroy himself in another way, for he must seem a traitor to the Volscians now just as he has been to Rome. He chooses almost certain death as he yields to his mother and 'holds her by the hand, silent'. Aufidius, who is a very much better politician, knows how to stir Coriolanus to uncontrollable rage by calling him 'traitor' and 'boy', and so to whip up the hostility of the people of Antium, who cry, 'Tear him to pieces'. He dies in his own image 'like an eagle', boasting of his soldiership, but also as a boy in tears, the child of his mother, who,

> fond of no second brood,
> Has cluck'd thee to the wars, and safely home,
> Loaden with honour.

(V.iii.162)

After showing himself in his changes of allegiance as fickle as the mob he hated for their instability, he makes in the end the best decision, the choice which rescues our sympathy for him, by framing 'convenient peace'. In doing so he relinquishes the old martial values for which he had stood, the stance of the 'lonely dragon', and accepts a political settlement. There is no place for him in this world, and it is fitting that he should die alone, in the centre of an angry mob.

In this play, as Aufidius says:

> our virtues
> Lie in th'interpretation of the time,

(IV.vii.49)

and the virtues of Coriolanus suit an older, more barbaric time, when martial strength and absolute rule were appropriate. Here the contrast with Hamlet is notable. Hamlet too has the virtues of an older time, but in his case not only are those virtues established as chivalric and in themselves attractive, but also absolutely as superior to the values prevailing in the court of Denmark; Claudius's world of diplomacy is shown as corrupt, and Hamlet,

G

The courtier's, soldier's, scholar's eye, tongue, sword,
Th'expectancy and rose of the fair state,

(III.i.151)

carries us with him as the good man cleansing what is 'rotten' in his country. The terms are changed in *Coriolanus*, in which all values are relative; the hero's virtues and values, splendid as these are in some ways, are simply out of place in an age moving towards civility, democracy and diplomacy as a way of conducting affairs. One way of describing the tragedy of Coriolanus would be to say that he cannot adapt himself to a changing society, and so is unable to fulfil the political role that society offers him.

If this is to point to the sense in which *Hamlet* is a moral tragedy and *Coriolanus* a political tragedy, it is also to draw attention to other important differences. *Coriolanus* might be seen as Shakespeare's adaptation to his own purposes of the new mood in tragedy represented in *Sejanus* and *The Revenger's Tragedy*. The hero is distanced from us by his own words and by the commentary of others upon him, and we are prevented from giving to him the kind of moral assent and warm loyalty of sympathy we give to Hamlet. He is conceived not primarily in moral terms, but in psychological terms, and as Antony will to his Egyptian dish again because he cannot help himself, so Coriolanus cannot help being what he is and earning his banishment in a monstrous integrity of pride. It is his nature to be thus, and though it might be said of him, as it is of Antony, that 'his taints and honours Wag'd equal with him' (V.i.30), we see both of these less in terms of a moral assessment than in terms of a psychological inadequacy or compulsion. They clash with the social order, with history, not like Hamlet and Lear with cosmic forces, the gods, heaven and hell. The later tragedies of Shakespeare are all like *Coriolanus* in recalling something of the tonality of the dark comedies, as suggested by the words of the First Lord in *All's Well*, 'The web of our life is of a mingled yarn, good and ill together'. They compensate for the distancing of the hero and a loss of moral urgency with a new realism, a more 'dispassionate and scientific scrutiny of life'.[1]

---

[1] The phrase is from Ian Watt's *The Rise of the Novel* (Berkeley and Los Angeles, 1957), p. 11. Some of the argument here is taken from my essay 'Shakespeare's Later Tragedies', printed in *Shakespeare 1564-1964*, edited by Edward A. Bloom

The effect in *Coriolanus* of the 'dominance of character over what we would like to be, of the priority of personality to principle in the motivation of human action' has been seen as rather depressing.[2] In showing things as they are rather than as they might be, the play is certainly not consoling, but neither is it bleak. The action allows us to respond simultaneously to the nobility and to the inadequacy of those possible centres of values which are suggested on a general level in the idea of the grandeur that was Rome, and on a personal level in the qualities of Coriolanus as a hero. Rome, the seat of civilization, is almost ruined by petty internal quarrels; Coriolanus, the triumphant warrior, is shown as vulnerable, unable either to fulfil his mother's desire and take on the role of politician, or to carry out his own wish and act as a punitive god. We are made conscious of the limitations of the society and the man, but the tough honesty with which they are shown enables us to respect and admire, firmly within limits, the greatness of both. It also points the way to a new exploitation of techniques for distancing characters and action. The late tragedies, as exemplified by *Coriolanus*, form a natural link between the dark comedies and the last plays.

(Providence, 1964), pp. 95-109. A. P. Riemer's book *A Reading of Shakespeare's 'Antony and Cleopatra'* (Sydney, 1968) analyses this play from a similar point of view, emphasizing its 'essential detachment' and Shakespeare's concern in it with 'things as they are, in the society of men, in the world of actual and tangible reality' (pp. 101, 114). I am aware of the degree to which 'All Shakespeare's plays show him keenly aware of the processes of audience engagement', as Maynard Mack has well argued, emphasizing the early and middle plays, in his 'Engagement and Detachment in Shakespeare's Plays' in *Essays on Shakespeare and Elizabethan Drama in Honour of Hardin Craig*, edited by Richard Hosley (1963), pp. 275-96; but an understanding of the ways in which modes of detachment are exploited by the dramatist in the late tragedies and the last plays is of basic importance if the nature of these plays is to be grasped.

[2] Norman Rabkin, 'Coriolanus: The Tragedy of Politics', *Shakespeare Quarterly* XVII (1966), p. 210. He goes on to say, 'Having dismayed us with the suggestion that principle – the only way to live admirably – must lead to ruin, Shakespeare will not allow us to find consolation in the thought that defeated principle at least has its integrity'. The idea that principle provides the only way to live admirably is precisely what this play rejects; principles themselves may, of course, be misguided, or lead to misery and evil in a rigid application, but *Coriolanus* goes further to suggest the idea of a psychological whole man, rather than a greatly good one, a flexible rather than an absolute man, and these qualities too may help us to 'live admirably'.

4

Shakespeare's last plays

(i) INTRODUCTION

In the dark comedies Shakespeare experimented with discontinuities and contradictions in character and action, withdrawing from the basic commitment to romantic love and to common ethical attitudes shown in the earlier comedies. In his late tragedies he withdrew from the moral commitment to good in its clash with evil which forms the basis of the central tragedies, learned how to distance his heroes, and to present them in terms of psychological necessity rather than moral discrimination. In his last plays Shakespeare seems to extend into a new kind of comedy the techniques developed in these two groups of plays. I call them comedies, for the term 'tragicomedy' is liable to mislead people into thinking of these plays as conceived in terms of a 'blending of tragedy and comedy in the right amounts',[1] when in fact their drive to establish what Guarini called 'the comic order' is clear from the start.[2] However, the dispassionate, primarily psychological treatment of character noticed in the

---

[1] The phrase is from the Introduction by J. M. Nosworthy to *Cymbeline* (New Arden edition, 1955), p. 1.

[2] In his *Compendium of Tragicomic Poetry* (1601); in a famous passage, translated in A. H. Gilbert, *Literary Criticism from Plato to Dryden* (1940), p. 511, Guarini stresses that in spite of the elements it borrows from tragedy, tragicomedy must reveal 'above all the comic order'.

late tragedies feeds into the last plays, in which characters tend to be given, not explained or motivated. So, for instance, the jealousy of Leontes is presented as a given fact about his nature, something he cannot help rather than a morally blameworthy condition of mind. But whereas Shakespeare made Coriolanus and Antony psychologically consistent, he exploits contradictions and discontinuities in the last plays, as is seen in the sudden change in Leontes himself, or in the presentation of figures like Cloten or Camillo. He combines techniques learned in earlier plays to create a dramatic world in which human intentions, the will, the act of choice, play a very subdued role, and actions by characters are referable to a psychological condition or compulsion, or to chance, or the influence of an uncertain heaven.

To put this another way, and focus it more sharply in terms of the action of these plays, it may help to consider as a particular point of reference the treatment of death. In the central tragedies deaths may be cataclysmic, involving the fate of nations, the return of chaos in the universe, and a prolonged intense suffering; the effort of the play is to magnify the effects and consequences of death, and makes us feel in the death of the older Hamlet, or of Duncan, or of Cordelia, an event that shatters peace and breaks hearts; Macbeth not only kills Duncan, he murders sleep. The death of Coriolanus is more muted, but still treated with ceremony as a matter of consequence. The earlier comedies usually start off from some threat of death, which provides an undertone to the plays, but is readily averted. Only in the last plays does Shakespeare effectively diminish the impact of death. The deaths of Cloten and the Queen in *Cymbeline*, like those of Mamillius and Antigonus in *The Winter's Tale*, occur casually, and pass with little notice. Cloten is slain by Guiderius, and Antigonus eaten by a bear, but no one is much troubled by these things, for they are presented within the detached perspective of a dramatic structure which treats death as a detail in the pattern of existence. A helpful comparison may be made with those paintings of the Renaissance in which some disaster, or a great historical or religious event, the ostensible subject of the picture, is treated in one corner of the canvas, while a landscape full of common activities of human life dominates the whole. W. H.

Auden seizes on the effect in his poem, 'Musée des Beaux Arts':

About suffering they were never wrong,
The Old Masters: how well they understood
Its human position; how it takes place
While someone else is eating or opening a window or just
    walking dully along;
How, when the aged are reverently, passionately waiting
For the miraculous birth, there always must be
Children who did not specially want it to happen, skating
On a pond at the edge of the wood:
They never forgot
That even the dreadful martyrdom must run its course
Anyhow in a corner, some untidy spot
Where the dogs go on with their doggy life, and the
    torturer's horse
Scratches its innocent behind on a tree.

In Brueghel's *Icarus*, for instance: how everything turns away
Quite leisurely from the disaster; the ploughman may
Have heard the splash, the forsaken cry,
But for him it was not an important failure; the sun shone
As it had to on the white legs disappearing into the green
Water; and the expensive delicate ship that must have seen
Something amazing, a boy falling out of the sky,
Had somewhere to get to and sailed calmly on.

The museum of Auden's title is in Brussels, and he was thinking especially of two paintings by Peter Brueghel the elder, one
of the gathering at Bethlehem at the time of the birth of Christ,
the other of the fall of Icarus. Brueghel shows both these great
events, a birth and a death, as details in the pictures; while a
handful of people crowd round a tiny shack where a miraculous
birth is taking place, tax-collectors are at work, and children
carelessly tumble and skate on frozen ponds; and Icarus is
barely noticeable as a leg vanishing into the sea, while in the
foreground on land a ploughman carries on with his work as if
nothing else matters. These paintings show a world in which
death and birth, suffering and miracle, are no more significant
than other human activities; one has to look hard to observe
them at all, and their reduction in scale diminishes their significance so that they seem no more and no less important than
other events.

The world of the last plays, especially *Cymbeline* and *The Winter's Tale* (for *The Tempest*, as I shall argue, leads off in new directions, even though it shares some of the characteristics of the two earlier plays) may be illuminated by this comparison. For it, too, is a world where things happen inexplicably or fortuitously, as it seems to the characters, where at any moment one may cry, 'thou met'st with things dying, I with things new-born', as simply the way life goes on. The schemes and intentions of men do not control the action, and at the same time, suffering, though sharply felt and often present, is a detail in the total pattern. Dramatically the last plays embody such a view of human existence. They emphasize event, however strange yet true, for its own sake, and merely as happening, to be accepted; what happens is apprehended as fact, not as an occasion for moralizing, and not in terms of causes and consequences. The reaction of the shepherds to the death of Antigonus in *The Winter's Tale* provides a notable instance of this; they simply accept what they find, a bear killing a man, a storm at sea destroying ship and crew, and a richly clothed body left at random on the shore. If these events have meaning, it is not in relation to the characters as such, but rather in relation to a patterning of human affairs by an agency which remains inscrutable to them. In accordance with this, the characters are not typically figures burdened by the anguish of motive, choice and responsibility; they tend to be given, not explained, and they can surprise us by their changes and adaptations to circumstance, just as the world they inhabit is full of accidents and coincidences. So, for example, the notorious inconsistencies of speech and behaviour in a figure like Cloten appear natural if we accept the basic dramatic conventions of the play; they exist not as a problem, or an unsatisfactory artifice, but as an aspect of event, as part of the mystery of human behaviour in an inexplicable world.

Those techniques for distancing the action and characters, and disengaging our sympathies and moral commitment, which Shakespeare developed in the dark comedies and his late tragedies, had to be extended for the last plays. Shakespeare did this most notably by making us continually aware of the incredible fictiveness of the action, by exposing what he is doing with a conscious and often blatant theatricality, as when

Jupiter creaks down on a property eagle, or an actor imitates a bear, or, in *The Tempest*, much of the play is shaped by Prospero's 'art'. At the same time the characters accept what happens without question, however odd it is, so that their calm assurance of the 'truth' of the sequence of events which crowd the plays with incident is set against our consciousness of the theatrical artifice. This is one aspect of the effect of paradox achieved by plays, inviting above all the reaction of wonder, as they seem directly to mediate the given condition of man as himself varying and contradictory, and subject to whim and accident in a world that offers no immediate explanations for its shifts and reversals.[1]

(ii) *Cymbeline*

Cymbeline begins with the entry of two gentlemen, who praise Posthumus glowingly, describe his ancestry, and report the loss of the King's two sons twenty years ago. The First Gentleman explains to his ignorant companion how Imogen has married against her father's wishes, a tough line of action in Shakespeare's time, how she has been imprisoned, her husband banished, and how, in spite of searching, the King's sons still remain untraced. It all sounds unlikely, but the Second Gentleman is convinced as his partner cries, 'Howso'er 'tis strange...Yet is it true, sir'. Already these figures begin to establish the tonality of the play, as one in which the strange, even the

[1] The argument here is based on my essay, 'Character and Dramatic Technique in *Cymbeline* and *The Winter's Tale*', printed in *Studies in the Arts*, edited by Francis Warner (Oxford, 1968), pp. 116-30. I had completed this book before I was able to see Norman Rabkin's important study, *Shakespeare and the Common Understanding* (New York, 1967). I find I share some of Mr Rabkin's basic attitudes; in his section on the last plays, he also stresses their 'theatrical self-consciousness', and the use in them of devices that 'call attention to the illusion' (pp. 215, 216). In addition, he finely observes how 'the people of Shakespeare's last imaginary worlds are at the mercy of forces, both internal and external, which they think they understand, but over which their control, tenuous at best, works only in ways beyond their comprehension' (p. 219). Mr Rabkin's argument is interesting and often subtle, but his primary concern is with themes; so *Cymbeline* and *The Winter's Tale* are both seen as tragedies mitigated or redeemed at the end, while Prospero is briefly accounted for as surrogate playwright, Shakespeare bidding farewell to his art, and *Henry VIII* is dismissed as a play Shakespeare did not take seriously. So an argument that begins brilliantly and seems to offer new challenges to our understanding of the plays, tends to resolve itself finally into a conventional reading of them.

incredible, will prove true, so that normal expectations of probability, consistency and motivation may not apply.

The action that follows is of a piece with the opening scene. The Queen, Imogen's wicked stepmother, hovering malignantly over her, and brewing strange concoctions out of herbs, might have stepped out of a fairy-tale. The unexpected intervention of Iachimo, whose villainy springs from within him, not from any motive against Posthumus and Imogen, takes us for a while into Renaissance Rome. At the court of Cymbeline, a British king, the Queen's son, Cloten, who appears as a clown in I.iii, mysteriously retains the favour of the King. Soon ancient Romans arrive at Milford Haven to invade Britain, and one might well ask why at Milford, of all places the most remote, unless it is to enable Imogen to make a long journey into Wales.[1] More surprises follow, for in Wales, Cloten, and Imogen, and we, by some almost incredible chance, encounter Belarius and the King's lost sons. So all is prepared for a final act in which Romans and British do battle; Posthumus, who, virtually single-handed, has saved the British, is arrested because he is in Roman costume, and gaoled by Cymbeline; and a whole series of discoveries is necessary to unravel the plot. These include the sudden death of the Queen, who is said to have misled Cymbeline; the recovery of Imogen, who has been masquerading as Fidele, the page of the Roman general, Lucius; the confession by Iachimo that he tricked Posthumus; the identification of Cymbeline's prisoner as Posthumus, and as the soldier who fought for the British; the establishment of Pisanio's loyalty to Imogen; the announcement to all of the death of Cloten; the discovery that Belarius is old Morgan, and that Guiderius and Arviragus are really Polydore and Cadwal, the King's lost sons; and, finally, the resubmission of Cymbeline to Rome.

This rough outline of the action shows that it could be summed up in terms similar to those used earlier of Marston's

---

[1] In an interesting essay, 'History and Histrionics in *Cymbeline*', *Shakespeare Survey*, 11 (1958), pp. 42-9, J. P. Brockbank seeks to support G. Wilson Knight in treating *Cymbeline* mainly as an historical play. This element is important, for the play is, in one sense, a chronicle, and an advance in this respect on *Pericles*. But it is pressing the point too hard to find, for example, a link between Lucius landing at Milford Haven, and the arrival there of Richmond in *Richard III* to free England from tyranny; but see Emrys Jones, 'Stuart Cymbeline', *Essays in Criticism*, XI (1961), 84-99.

Antonio and Mellida as an impossible fiction composed of some of 'the silliest elements known to Elizabethan drama'.[1] The analogy would be superficial, for Shakespeare's purpose is very different from Marston's, but it draws attention to an important fact about both plays, their deliberate use of the most disparate materials in an obviously contrived way. In *Cymbeline*, as the final scene with its series of surprising discoveries indicates, the interest does not lie in the development of character, or of plot in the sense of a developing action with a beginning, a middle or crisis, and end, or resolution, like that, say, of *Othello* or *Coriolanus*. Instead, we are offered a multiplicity of plots and a continual variety in unexpected twists to the action; the *unexpected*, indeed, seems a necessary part of the play's movement, and of the pattern of expectations it sets up. It invites us to look not for what is probable, or for a motivated, consequential action, but rather to accept the most extraordinary coincidences and accidents, and to be ready to respond with an assent like that of the First Gentleman, 'Howso'er 'tis strange. . . . Yet is it true'.

If we accept the tonality of the play as indicated in the opening scenes, then other assumptions and conventions become clearer. Flagrant improbabilities are taken for granted, such as that in a journey across Wales, both Cloten and Imogen would stumble into the exact spot where Belarius has hidden untraced for twenty years; or that Lucius, the Roman ambassador, would be in need of an attendant at that precise moment when Imogen happens to turn up in Milford Haven, and that he would hire her, in her disguise as a boy, on sight. There are many more such instances, which Shakespeare clearly was at pains to expose, and not to conceal. Of a piece with these is the overt display of theatricality.[2] No attempt is made to create a consistent illusion of human beings in action as Shakespeare lays bare, sometimes with what looks like deliberate crudeness, intricacies of the action in a creakingly theatrical way. This begins early with the asides to the audience of the Second Lord

---

[1] See above, p. 40. The quotation is from G. K. Hunter's Introduction to *Antonio and Mellida*, p. xii.

[2] Arthur C. Kirsch has commented on the play's 'self-conscious contrivance' in his important essay on '*Cymbeline* and Coterie Dramaturgy', *ELH*, XXXIV (1967), 285-306. See also F. Kermode, *Shakespeare; The Final Plays* (1963), pp. 21-2.

in I.iii, recommending us to note what a fool Cloten is, and the asides in I.vi, when Cornelius the doctor gives a box of drugs to the Queen. Here both characters, and Pisanio, who comes in midway through the scene, have asides or short soliloquies in which they appear to come downstage to address the audience directly, perhaps concealing their words from the other characters with a melodramatic gesture. The asides have a function, and provide information, but they seem to be used in a deliberately obtrusive way, as if to make us notice the theatrical device. So, as Pisanio enters, the Queen and Cornelius in turn speak in aside:

> Queen   [*Aside*] Here comes a flattering rascal, upon him
> Will I first work: he's for his master,
> And enemy to my son. – How now Pisanio? –
> Doctor, your service for this time is ended,
> Take your way.
> Cornelius   [*Aside*] I do suspect you, madam;
> But you shall do no harm.
>
>   (I.v.27)

A similar kind of effect is produced when, as happens from time to time, characters sum up the story so far as it has gone, or have a little choric speech, as if to remind us of what, in the complications of intrigue, we may have half-forgotten, like Imogen at the opening of I.vi:

> A father cruel, and a step-dame false,
> A foolish suitor to a wedded lady,
> That hath her husband banished . . .

Here she sums up the situation for us, much as does the Second Lord when he suddenly breaks out in a verse soliloquy at the end of II.i:

> Thou divine Imogen, what thou endur'st,
> Betwixt a father by thy step-dame govern'd,
> A mother hourly coining plots, a wooer
> More hateful than the foul expulsion is
> Of thy dear husband, than that horrid act
> Of the divorce he'ld make. The heavens hold firm
> The walls of thy dear honour, keep unshak'd
> That temple, thy fair mind, that thou mayst stand
> T'enjoy thy banish'd lord, and this great land!
>
>   (II.i.55)

Again this Lord outlines the action and projects a happy outcome, but it is a gratuitous speech, not arising in any way from
the preceding action. The Second Lord's sole function hitherto
has been to abuse Cloten. Perhaps the most notable example of
such gratuitous speech occurs with the introduction of Belarius
in III.iii. We were told a little about him in the opening scene
of the play, but now Shakespeare amplifies the details without
troubling to disguise what he is doing. The conversation between
Belarius and the boys Guiderius and Arviragus turns on the
difference between court and country, nature and nurture; the
boys not unreasonably feel rather irritated at living among
animals, and knowing nothing of the benefits of civilization,
although they talk in accomplished blank verse, and in speech
might pass among the best, but Belarius explains as though for
the first time his dislike of the court, and then repeats his life
story, all of which one might think superfluous after twenty
years of living together. But if the boys have heard it before,
we have not, and Shakespeare put it there for us. At the end of
the scene, Belarius sends the boys off to hunt, and finishes with
a soliloquy filling out some details we have not yet heard:

> O Cymbeline, heaven and my conscience knows
> Thou didst unjustly banish me: whereon
> At three and two years old, I stole these babes,
> Thinking to bar thee of succession as
> Thou reft'st me of my lands. Euriphile,
> Thou wast their nurse, they took thee for their mother,
> And every day do honour to her grave:
> Myself, Belarius, that am Morgan call'd,
> They take for natural father.

(III.iii.99)

Belarius here speaks for the benefit of the audience, imparting
information directly, and the soliloquy springs not from the
action, or from introspection, but is presented as narrative.
Shakespeare adopted in this scene a direct narrative means of
supplying some facts with complete disregard for probability
or character conceived as psychologically consistent. Belarius
is simply used for the moment as a kind of chorus.

Probably at any stage of his career, and certainly now in his
maturity, Shakespeare could have worked this material into
the action more subtly if he had wished to do so; the only

reasonable way to explain it is to suppose that it was a deliberate tactic on his part.[1] It is of a piece with other aspects of the play, some of which have been noted above, in drawing attention to itself as theatrical device. The aim seems to have been to make us think less of the character and more of the actor speaking from a stage. It may be seen as one means of preventing us from identifying ourselves with a character, or taking the action too seriously, at any rate on a literal level. The famous stage direction in Act V for Jupiter to descend 'in thunder and lightning, sitting upon an eagle', and to throw a thunderbolt, a direction which the nature of the text encourages us to suppose is Shakespeare's own, provides another example of deliberate emphasis on theatrical effect. Here the physical machinery of the stage is palpably employed, not for illusion, but for a piece of clever spectacle, as the god comes down, lowered presumably on wires, and then vanishes aloft into what Sicilius calls his 'radiant roof' (V.iv.121) in the canopy or 'heavens' at the Globe.

The conscious theatricality shown here and elsewhere, as in the scene in Imogen's bedroom (II.ii) where the clock marks the passage of more than three hours in the space of forty lines, is related to the deliberate emphasis on chance, accident, and the improbable, and both in turn are connected with the presentation of characters not as human beings conceived in terms of psychological consistency, but rather as liable to arbitrary shifts and changes. Shakespeare, it is true, treats the characters in different ways according to their function in the play; so, for instance, Pisanio remains throughout a stock figure, the devoted loyal servant of Imogen and Posthumus, and neither changes nor develops. The point is that, given the deliberately arbitrary nature of the action, as not dependent on cause and motive, and as flaunting its theatricality and rejection of ordinary narrative continuity and expectation, there is no need for a stable and consistent portrayal and development of characters; they may be liberated from consistency, since they too are part of a dramatic world where anything can happen, however strange, yet true.

---

[1] H. Granville-Barker noted some of these features and, puzzled by them, supposed another hand than Shakespeare's was to be found in the play; he asked, 'Can we see Shakespeare, past-master of his craft, making such a mess of the job?' (*Prefaces to Shakespeare*, Second Series, 1930, p. 238).

Consider, for example, Cloten. When we first see him, in I.iii and II.i, he is accompanied by two lords; one of them feeds him with lines, while the other speaks almost continually in asides to the audience, inviting us to think of Cloten as a fool or ass, and mocking him:

Cloten	When a gentleman is dispos'd to swear, it is not for any standers-by to curtail his oaths, ha?
Second Lord	No, my lord; [*Aside*] nor crop the ears of them.
Cloten	Whoreson dog! I give him satisfaction? Would he had been one of my rank!
Second Lord	[*Aside*] To have smelt like a fool.
Cloten	I am not vex'd more at anything in th' earth; a pox on't! I had rather not be so noble as I am. . . .

(II.i.10)

This rough prose is characteristic of Cloten's speeches in these scenes; he behaves as a foolishly arrogant prince, occupied in quarrelling, playing bowls and gambling, who appears to justify the comment of the Second Lord when he is left alone on stage to address the audience at the end of II.i:

That such a crafty devil as is his mother
Should yield the world this ass! a woman that
Bears all down with her brain, and this her son
Cannot take two from twenty, for his heart,
And leave eighteen.

(II.i.50)

Shortly afterwards, in II.iii, Cloten attempts to woo Imogen, in a scene which brings him on again with the lords, and speaking in prose; it is the old Cloten here who shows no feeling for the exquisite song 'Hark, hark the lark', yet a few lines later, when he is left alone to knock at her door, his speech changes into blank verse of some power:

I know her women are about her: what
If I do line one of their hands? 'Tis gold
Which buys admittance (oft it doth) yea, and makes
Diana's rangers false themselves, yield up
Their deer to th'stand o'th'stealer; and 'tis gold
Which makes the true-man kill'd, and saves the thief,
Nay, sometime hangs both thief and true-man; what

Can it not do and undo? I will make
One of her women lawyer to me, for
I yet not understand the case myself.

(II.iii.66)

Cloten here begins suddenly to speak in a music that echoes
Lear or Timon:

This yellow slave
Will knit and break religions; bless th'accurs'd;
Make the hoar leprosy ador'd, place thieves,
And give them title, knee and approbation
With senators on the bench.

(*Timon of Athens*, IV.iii.33)

The contrast with Cloten's earlier manner has led critics to see
here a lapse of dramatic integrity, or an 'inconsistent and even
contradictory' portrayal of character.[1]

An attempt has been made to account for this speech within
a reading of the play as 'definable in symbolic terms', that is to
say treating character and plot as 'simply an extension, and
extra vehicle of the poetry'.[2] Then Cloten's lines may seem to
be relevant to a 'general conception' of the play:[3]

The manner of expression here has its significance for the
general conception. The idea of chastity is bound up with an
allusive, self-conscious artifice – 'Diana's rangers' – which is
again not without relation to Iachimo's recent words in
Imogen's bedroom. Decorative as it is in feeling, it conceals
the corrupt motives which underline Cloten's barely disguised
animality; and this in turn naturally accepts the idea of corruption (*false* themselves'), turns on the related ideas of legal-
ity and bribery, involves 'thief and trueman' alike in the
promiscuous confusion of values. Here, once more we are in
the presence of the artificial, egoistic and brutal world from
which Imogen needs to escape. . . .

---

[1] Granville-Barker, *op. cit.*, p. 290; see also J. M. Nosworthy's Introduction to
the New Arden edition, p. lvii. In the more recent New Cambridge edition of
Cymbeline (1960), the editor, J. C. Maxwell, points to Granville-Barker's account
of the play as 'the most helpful exploration of Shakespeare's methods in it'
(p. xxxii).
[2] Derek Traversi, *Shakespeare; The Last Phase* (1954), pp. 2 and 3. At this point
he is describing his approach to the last plays as a group.
[3] *Ibid.*, p. 59.

The trouble with this analysis is that a notion of consistency of symbolic status for Cloten replaces a notion of consistency of character; Cloten cannot be allowed the employment of his attractive image of Diana, goddess of chastity, without being accused of concealing corrupt motives, when his purpose is plain enough. The note of heavy-handed moral indignation in this account of Cloten's speech seems to miss the point. He is attempting to buy the help of a waiting-woman in order to gain access to Imogen, and the idea of the power of gold to corrupt is a truism echoed in many plays of the age:

> Riches, the dumb god, that giv'st all men tongues:
> Thou canst do nought, and yet mak'st men do all things;
> The price of souls; even hell, with thee to boot,
> Is made worth heaven. Thou art virtue, fame,
> Honour, and all things else.
>
> (Jonson, Volpone, I.i.22)

The remarkable thing is that Cloten's poetry rings with an authority similar to that of Timon and Volpone; for the moment he appears wise in the ways of the world, and speaks with dignity. The image of 'Diana's rangers' is entirely appropriate to the sort of high rhetoric Cloten speaks here, besides being a kind of indirect compliment to Imogen, whose 'rangers' he hopes to bribe; but it is quite out of keeping with the prosy, foolish clown of the earlier scenes, who, as the Second Lord assured us, could not take two from twenty.

When Shakespeare wants Cloten to speak with grace and intelligence, he has him do so, however inconsistent it may be. So later on Cloten addresses the Roman ambassador, Lucius, with a warlike simplicity as if he were some noted fighter in an earlier history play:

> His majesty bids you welcome. Make pastime with us a day
> or two, or longer: if you seek us afterwards in other terms,
> you shall find us in our salt-water girdle; if you beat us out of
> it, it is yours; if you fall in the adventure, our crows shall fare
> the better for you, and there's an end.
>
> (III.i.76

The old arrogant fool returns in III.v, as Cloten sets off to Wales in lustful pursuit of Imogen. He is not presented as a stable or psychologically consistent figure, but this is neither a failure on Shakespeare's part to work out a consistent mode of treating him, nor is it explicable in symbolic terms. It seems rather that Shakespeare was moving in *Cymbeline* towards a mode of drama which could abandon the idea of character as morally or psychologically stable, and one result is the presence of figures like Cloten, who changes from scene to scene, and is given a variety of styles of speech to match the varying and even contradictory versions of him we see. In other words, he is not revealed at once in a mode of speech that gives us in some sense the hallmark of the man, like Hamlet, Othello, or Coriolanus, but is conceived in a more flexible way, and changes with the situation; alone with his followers he appears a quarrelsome fool, but he can speak verse of distinction when thinking of Imogen, and he challenges the Romans in good plain sensible English.

Although Cloten provides the most notable instance of such 'inconsistency', he is not alone in being presented in this way. The Queen, for example, drops her witch-like, conspiratorial manner to become the champion of England, echoing John of Gaunt, as she stiffens Cymbeline's opposition to Rome:

> Remember, sir, my liege,
> The kings your ancestors, together with
> The natural bravery of your isle, which stands
> As Neptune's park, ribb'd and pal'd in
> With rocks unscaleable and roaring waters,
> With sands that will not bear your enemies' boats,
> But suck them up to th' topmast . . .
>
> (III.i.16)

The sudden transformation of Posthumus from eternally faithful lover to hater of all women upon hearing Iachimo's account of Imogen relates to this variation in the presentation of characters, and to the arbitrary features of action and dialogue, and instances of overt theatricality noted earlier. The presentation of the central figures, Imogen and Posthumus, is more subtle and complicated than that of Cloten or the Queen, but they all need to be understood in relation to the pattern of expectations established from the beginning; the mode of the play, its variations and mingling of conventions, seems designed, among

H

other things, to make us accept what happens as in some sense
'true', and at the same time to prevent us from committing
ourselves to any one character.

A subtle distancing operates in respect of Imogen and
Posthumus. They begin the play in the unusual, indeed unique
position for Shakespeare's romantic heroes and heroines, of
being married. They are at first so perfect, so much the 'loyalest
husband' and wife, that they may seem to be almost over-acting
their love, and the echo in their parting protestations of the
leave-taking between Troilus and Cressida, is probably deliberate. For Imogen, who idealizes her husband as one who 'over-
buys me Almost the sum he pays' (I.i.146), their parting seems
an opportunity for acting out prettily the most romantic of
farewells; she is less absorbed in Posthumus than in her imagin-
ings of how she might have watched him go:

> I would have broke mine eye-strings, crack'd them, but
> To look upon him, till the diminution
> Of space had pointed him, sharp as my needle,
> Nay, follow'd him, till he had melted from
> The smallness of a gnat to air, and then
> Have turn'd mine eye, and wept.

> (I.iii.17)

She would have wept if the separation could have been so staged,
but at the actual parting there are no tears. There the hurried
nature of the parting in the presence of the Queen shortens
their speeches, and controls their feeling, which becomes simple
and moving, especially in Imogen's:

> O the gods!
> When shall we see again?

> (I.i.124)

After this, however, each is shown as lacking in true knowledge
of and feeling for the other, with the result that Posthumus
becomes passionate in hatred and thoughts of vengeance, while
Imogen becomes sentimental and at times almost comic.

At the first test of his love, Posthumus, who goes about
boasting of his wife's excelling beauty and virtue, believes a
complete stranger's testimony that she is disloyal. It might
perhaps be thought a hollow confidence in Imogen that drives
Posthumus to brag so much that she is 'more fair, virtuous,

wise, chaste, constant, qualified, and less attemptable' than the rarest ladies of France (I.iv.57), to quarrel at swordpoint, and then to accept Iachimo's wager rashly; if not hollow, then it is slightly absurd, for it indicates the extent to which she has been for him an idea rather than a person, an embodiment of chastity too pure for common mortality; and when this idea of her is made distasteful to him by Iachimo, he casts her off readily, without even hearing out the evidence:

> Let there be no honour
> Where there is beauty; truth, where semblance; love,
> Where there's another man. The vows of women
> Of no more bondage be to where they are made
> Than they are to their virtues, which is nothing.
> O, above measure false!

(II.iv.108)

Iachimo's possession of Imogen's ring is enough to make him translate his love for her into hatred for all women. In a parallel way, Imogen loves an idea of heroism rather than a person, as is shown when Iachimo, who has just insulted her as outrageously as possible by treating her as a potential prostitute, and who has slandered her husband as a profligate, wins her over with equally outrageous flattery of him:

> he is one
> The truest manner'd; such a holy witch
> That he enchants societies into him.
> Half all men's hearts are his.
>
> *Imogen*   You make amends.
> *Iachimo* He sits 'mongst men like a descended god;
> He hath a kind of honour sets him off
> More than a mortal seeming.

(I.vi.164)

This is what Imogen loves to hear, and it ensures Iachimo's welcome:

All's well, sir; take my power i'th'court for yours.

Imogen is content to think of Posthumus as like a god, and knows him as little as he knows her. Shakespeare presents her as full of pretty speeches and tender sentiments appropriate to her situation, but with an edge of comic irony in what she says, and a tendency to overdo the part a little bit, and strain across the boundary of the absurd. When she hears that Posthumus is in Milford Haven, she would leap to horse to join him, without pausing to find out how far away Milford is; her faith in him is touching, and her final urgency in this scene is fine:

> I see before me, man; nor here, nor here,
> Nor what ensues, but have a fog in them,
> That I cannot look through.
>
> (III.ii.77)

However, this follows on a sequence in which she receives his letter, spends fifteen lines hoping for good news before opening it, and then with a conscious rhetoric addresses Pisanio:

> Then, true Pisanio,
> Who long'st, like me, to see thy lord; who long'st
> (O let me bate) but not like me, yet long'st,
> But in a fainter kind. O, not like me,
> For mine's beyond beyond. Say, and speak thick
> (Love's counsellor should fill the bores of hearing
> To th' smothering of the sense) how far it is
> To this same blessed Milford.
>
> (III.ii.51)

It is almost as if she is concerned to stage the scene in a way proper to romance, to moderate her ardour in representing Pisanio's attachment to her husband, and then to have him 'speak thick' in counselling her.

Two scenes later, when they are well on in their journey into Wales, Pisanio produces another letter from Posthumus, to elicit in her a different kind of reaction. This letter, commanding Pisanio to kill her, shatters her image of Posthumus, and she more than welcomes the idea of death, indeed, would kill herself but for the divine prohibition against such an act. Here again she seems prettily engaged in making the most of the scene; she draws the sword herself from the scabbard he is wearing, and offers it to him:

> I draw the sword myself; take it, and hit
> The innocent mansion of my love, my heart:
> Fear not, 'tis empty of all things but grief. . . .
>
> (III.iv.65)

Pisanio refuses the offered sword, but still she presses him, pulling open her habit to expose her bosom, only to find that there is an impediment in the way: in concentrating on her performance as sacrificial lamb (she says later 'Prithee despatch. The lamb entreats the butcher'), she has forgotten that the mansion of her love is stuffed with the earlier letter of Posthumus:

> Come, here's my heart,
> (Something's afore it – soft, soft! we'll no defence)
> Obedient as the scabbard. What is here?
> The scriptures of the loyal Leonatus,
> All turn'd to heresy? Away, away,
> Corrupters of my faith! you shall no more
> Be stomachers to my heart. . . .

(III.iv.76)

Her failure to recall that there is something protecting her heart, and to remember what it is, provides some comic irony here, which is reinforced by the way her fancy plays about the situation. She imagines the letter as armour ('defence'), her heart as the scabbard for sheathing the blade, the letter as scripture, and then as a stomacher or article of clothing, all in rapid succession. The effect is to prevent us from taking the situation very seriously, for she is clearly not going to die at this point; but also it emphasizes the extent to which she is concerned to be to the full a betrayed woman and lamb for the slaughter, concerned, that is to say, for herself, rather as Posthumus was concerned for himself when he thought her false. The image of his 'scriptures' as 'turn'd to heresy' is appropriate in this connection, for she had worshipped an idol, and now her faith in men is destroyed, as his was in women; and as he was ready to believe Imogen a 'whore' on evidence, according to Philario, 'not strong enough to be believ'd Of one persuaded well of' (II.iv.131), so now, without any prompting from Pisanio, she imagines that godlike husband embracing another woman:

> I grieve myself
> To think, when thou shalt be disedg'd by her
> That now thou tirest on, how thy memory
> Will then be pang'd by me.

(III.iv.91)

The culmination of this process of rendering Imogen at once sympathetic and faintly comic comes when she awakes from her drugged sleep to find a body by her side clothed in the garments of Posthumus. She had earlier said to Cloten that the meanest garment of Posthumus was dearer to her 'than all the hairs' on him (II.iii.135) and she now takes the clothes for the man, and proceeds to itemize the body on assumption that it is Posthumus:

> A headless man? The garments of Posthumus?
> I know the shape of's leg; this is his hand;
> His foot Mercurial; his Martial thigh;
> The brawns of Hercules; but his Jovial face –
> Murder in heaven! How? – 'Tis gone.
>
> (IV.ii.309)

This episode is comic in several ways, because a number of incongruities are at work. Imogen shows how little she knows the husband whose limbs she thinks she recognizes, and here above all her ignorance of Posthumus is brought out. Now she thinks Posthumus dead, he recovers his godlike quality, and indeed, in her fancy becomes a combination of bits of various deities, Mercury, Mars, Hercules, Jupiter, all inappropriate to the image of Cloten, whose body is actually on stage. Also comic is the way she proceeds from the body to the head, with a kind of delayed recognition that the head is missing, which bursts out in the curious lines:

> O Posthumus, alas,
> Where is thy head? where's that? Ay me! where's that?
> Pisanio might have kill'd thee at the heart,
> And left this head on.
>
> (IV.ii.322)

Imogen's fancy expresses itself in a concern for the body as an assembly of parts, with the most important one, the head, missing; this is to reduce the body to a kind of mechanism, and her rhetoric here is absurd in itself. At the same time, though her logic is false and her rhetoric extravagant; though she is made to indulge her grief by again staging the scene, as when she smears herself with the blood of Cloten for the benefit of those who will find her:

This is Pisanio's deed, and Cloten – O!
Give colour to my pale cheek with thy blood,
That we the horrider may seem to those
Which chance to find us;

(IV.ii.330)

yet her anger with Pisanio and grief over the supposed death of
Posthumus are genuine.[1] Moreover, she has just been cere-
moniously laid to rest as dead by Belarius, Guiderius and
Arviragus, with expressions of their tender affection for her,
as a 'blessed thing' they associate with flowers and fairies
(IV.ii.207), and immediately afterwards she is found by Lucius,
who takes her, in her disguise as Fidele, into his service on mere
sight:

The Roman Emperor's letters
Sent by a consul to me should not sooner
Than thine own worth prefer thee.

(IV.ii.387)

The scene combines tenderness and humour, as if Shakespeare
wants to ensure that we watch the action with a degree of
amused detachment as well as sympathy. This is not to be confused with what happens in the early comedies, where we watch
the 'strange capers' of true lovers on their way through courtship to marriage, with the sense, in Touchstone's words, that
'as all is mortal in nature, so is all nature in love mortal in folly'

---

[1] Many see this episode as wholly serious, and as bringing 'the tragic complications to a crisis' (Marvin T. Herrick, *Tragicomedy*, 1955, p. 257); and a larger
thesis is widely accepted, namely that 'Each of Shakespeare's last plays opposes
extremes of virtue and vice; base treachery challenges the most shining loyalty,
but without tragic consequence because in each case, a harsh and threatening
actuality is miraculously transformed by the sundry operations of repentance,
faith, forbearance' (Cyrus Hoy, *The Hyacinth Room*, 1964, p. 271). It seems to
me that we do not for a moment expect a 'tragic consequence', but are alert to
the nature of an action which may be often comic, sometimes sad, but never
tragic; and moreover, virtue and vice, repentance and forbearance, are mislead-
ing terms for an action in which providence intervenes in acts of grace, and not
according to the nature or deserts of the characters. The special treatment of
character in the last plays was observed by F. R. Leavis in his incisive essay, 'The
Criticism of Shakespeare's Last Plays', *Scrutiny*, X (1941-2), 339-45. For an
interesting account of *Cymbeline* that emphasizes comic aspects of the play, see
F. D. Hoeniger, 'Irony and Romance in *Cymbeline*', *Studies in English Literature*,
II (1962), 219-28.

(*As You Like It*, II.iv.51); in these plays we are engaged sympathetically in watching the successful overcoming of all obstacles by young lovers, while at the same time having something of Puck's stance:

> Shall we their fond pageant see?
> Lord, what fools these mortals be!
> > (*A Midsummer Night's Dream*, III.ii.114)

In *Cymbeline* the effect is different, and the presentation of Imogen links with other features of the play described earlier to emphasize rather how subject to whim, chance, accident, mistaken judgments, and wild coincidences the pattern of existence is. When Imogen wakes from the sleep brought on by Pisanio's drug, she exclaims:

> I hope I dream;
> For so I thought I was a cave-keeper,
> And cook to honest creatures. But 'tis not so;
> 'Twas but a bolt of nothing, shot at nothing,
> Which the brain makes of fumes. Our very eyes
> Are sometimes like our judgments, blind.
> > (IV.ii.298)

This is not the 'blindness' or folly of lovers, symbolized in the magic juices Puck squeezes on to the eyelids of the lovers in *A Midsummer Night's Dream*, but has more far-reaching implications. Imogen thinks now that she merely dreamt what we have seen happen, her encounter with Belarius, Guiderius and Arviragus, who were not in any case the peasants she thought them. She takes the body on stage for that of Posthumus, when we know it is Cloten's. She has been buried as dead by Belarius and the king's sons, but we quickly discover that she is still alive. Belarius and the boys are disguised as Welsh mountaineers, Imogen is disguised as a boy, and Cloten's body is dressed in the clothes of Posthumus. Eyes and judgments are bound to deceive sometimes, in a world such as this.

Here some of the central contradictions in the world of *Cymbeline* are gathered, and the scene might be thought of as exemplifying, with a self-consciousness appropriate to the paradox, some of the oppositions brought together in those paradoxical exercises that were popular in the sixteenth and seventeenth centuries:[1]

> For fyrst it is not unknowen, how all humaine thynges . . .
> have two faces muche unlyke and dissemblable, that what
> outwardly seemed death, yet lokyng within ye shulde fynde
> it lyfe: and on the other side what semed life, to be death:
> what fayre, to be foule: what riche, beggerly: what cunnyng,
> rude: what stronge, feable: what noble, vile: what gladsome,
> sadde: what happie, unlucky: what friendly, unfriendly: what
> healthsome, noysome.

In *Cymbeline* these contradictions do not emerge in a confusion of the mind, like that of Macbeth or Lear, or, except incidentally, as a consequence or aspect of human folly, as this displays itself in the willed acts of human beings at cross-purposes – so, while the last plays of Shakespeare have clowns, none of them has that central figure of the earlier comedies, the fool, or mocking commentator on the acts and intentions of others. The contradictions and paradoxes in *Cymbeline* are there simply as a fact about human experience. The presentation of the action and characters tends to prevent us from thinking of causes, motives, moral confusions, purposes, and makes us attend rather to events as they happen, making us wonder at their strangeness.

Posthumus, like Imogen, is brought to recognize his own blindness, and to achieve liberty through bondage. After fighting disguised as a 'Briton peasant' (V.i.24), and aiding in the rescue of Cymbeline, he allows himself to be captured as a Roman, and thrust in gaol, as a kind of penitence for the death he thinks he has inflicted on Imogen; here he prays for his own death as the way to freedom:

> Most welcome bondage! for thou art a way
> I think, to liberty.

(V.iv.3)

As Imogen went through a kind of death after taking Pisanio's drug, so now Posthumus falls asleep as he prays the gods to

---

[1] Cited from Erasmus, *The Praise of Folly*, in the translation of Sir Thomas Chaloner (1549), edited by Clarence H. Miller (Early English Text Society, 1965), p. 37. See also Rosalie Colie, *Paradoxica Epidemica* (1966), for a full account of the use of paradoxes in Renaissance literature.

'take this life', and in a sense 'dies'. He has a dream-vision of his dead parents and brothers, and of Jupiter descending in thunder and sulphurous smoke on a golden eagle, which is marvellous to him, and still more so to the audience, who see an actual epiphany, the most extraordinary happening in a series of strange events. Posthumus had expected to go the way of final blindness, to death, saying, 'there are none want eyes to direct them the way I am going', but instead gains new sight; he had prayed for loss of life as freedom, and instead is 'call'd to be made free' indeed (V.iv.192). When he is reunited with Imogen at the end of the play, one theme of it is completed in that their eyes are opened, and we have the sense that they know one another and themselves a little better, and that their mutual love has been 'earned' in the test of hard adventures.

However, it is not something they have willed or worked for, but has rather been granted to them by accident, coincidence, and the intervention of Jupiter. The famous series of revelations, constantly bringing fresh confrontations and news of further strange coincidences, which forms the culmination of the action in the final scene, flows naturally out of what has gone before, and is in keeping with the tonality and mode of the whole. The revelations come as unexpected, not as caused by a chain of consequence. When Posthumus reports to one of the lords who has fled, with the King and entire British army, from the Romans, how he, with Belarius, 'an old man, and two boys', turned the battle and made the Romans withdraw routed, the lord expresses his admiration:

Lord	This was strange chance,
	A narrow lane, an old man, and two boys.
Posthumus	Nay, do not wonder at it; you are made
	Rather to wonder at the things you hear
	Than to work any.

(V.iii.52)

Posthumus is angry with the lord for being one of those who fled, and so one made to hear the wonders rather than to work them; but the audience is in something of the same position as the lord, in accepting with wonder the strange chances they see and hear enacted before them. The last scene begins with the unexpected news of the Queen's death, and continues with reports and discoveries that bring to light Iachimo's treachery, make Posthumus, Imogen, Belarius and the King's sons reveal themselves, and overwhelm Cymbeline with the constant stream of 'New matter still' (V.v.243). Again and again the news is good, bringing the restoration of what has been lost, turning peasant into prince, replacing discord with harmony, and offering peace in place of war, love in place of hate, forgiveness in place of malice. Cymbeline recovers his children, but not through any effort of his, and the deliverance from error and loss, which is also a kind of rebirth, comes as an unlooked for gift of providence; so Cymbeline cries:

> O, what am I?
> A mother to the birth of three? Ne'er mother
> Rejoic'd deliverance more. Blest pray you be
> That after this strange starting from your orbs,
> You may reign in them now!
>
> (V.v.368)

It is the mysterious operation of a providence not understood by the characters that brings restitution finally, and purges evil in the casual deaths of Cloten and the Queen. The structure of the play depends not on motive or causality or intention so much as on coincidence, chance, accident, which seem beyond man's control, and inexplicable, though accepted without question as an aspect of the nature of life. Providence manifests itself unexpectedly in Act V when Jupiter appears to Posthumus, and leaves on his bosom that 'book' or 'label' containing a prophecy the sense of which is pretty clear to the audience, though inscrutable to him. A soothsayer has to be called to explain it at the end, when the only part of the prophecy not fulfilled is the last phrase, that Britain shall 'flourish in peace and plenty' (V.v.440). Cymbeline at once takes upon himself the fulfilment of this as he submits to Rome, crying, 'My peace we will begin' (V.v.457). The presence of the 'covering heavens' is thus felt as:

> The fingers of the powers above do tune
> The harmony of this peace.
>
> (V.v.464)

The voluntary submission of Cymbeline here, and the ending of the play with prayer and praise of the gods, crowning all in harmony, arises out of the direct intervention of a god, Jupiter, in the play. Up to that point, there is nothing to explain the inconsistencies, contradictions, and coincidences of the action; and its deliberate theatricalities, self-consciousness in the presentation of characters, its devices for distancing them and avoiding a sense of psychological realism, among which may be included the bringing together of the ancient Britain of Cymbeline and the Renaissance Italy of Iachimo, all help to shape the play within an overall consistent and intelligible dramatic mode, in which the resolution can come not by the will of men, but only by the intervention of the heavens. Imogen wakes from her drugged sleep to think she has dreamt of meeting Belarius, Guiderius and Arviragus, and, waking to find a body by her, believes 'The dream's here still' (IV.ii.307); so Posthumus, emerging from a sleep which has brought the vision of Jupiter, finds the paper containing the prophecy laid on him, and thinks "Tis still a dream'. They confuse dream and actual existence because existence to them has in any case many of the qualities of a dream in its strangeness and its unexpected turns of event; and the overlap between dream and actuality is embodied for the audience too in the action, as Belarius and Jupiter are seen to be as 'real' as Imogen and Posthumus. The mode of the play is such as to make us, the audience, share something of Posthumus's puzzled acceptance of his 'dream' and prophecy:

> 'Tis still a dream; or else such stuff as madmen
> Tongue, and brain not; either both, or nothing,
> Or senseless speaking, or a speaking such
> As sense cannot untie. Be what it is,
> The action of my life is like it. . . .

> (V.iv.144)

He cannot make sense of the prophecy, which, whether it spring from dream or madness or whatever, remains inexplicable, yet somehow like the action of his life. In an analogous sense we may say of the play as a whole that it is like the action of our own lives.

(iii) *The Winter's Tale*

The Winter's Tale is in many respects a play very like *Cymbeline*, and clearly belongs to the same dramatic mode. Both plays begin with disaster; in *Cymbeline* the king banishes Posthumus and imprisons his daughter Imogen, apparently in a fit of anger, and without reference to his courtiers, who approve the marriage of Imogen and Posthumus:

> not a courtier,
> Although they wear their faces to the bent
> Of the king's looks, hath a heart that is not
> Glad at the thing they scowl at.
>
> (I.i.12)

They accept what has happened without surprise and without explanation. The king's violence, the outrage he would do on his own daughter, flows out of him like lightning, and seems far in excess of any cause:

> let her languish
> A drop of blood a day, and being aged,
> Die of this folly.
>
> (I.i.156)

His irrational behaviour may subsequently be linked with that 'wicked queen' (V.v.461) who, by the convenience of the heavens, dies suddenly just before the final revelations and restorations, confessing then how she hated Imogen and hoped to

> work
> Her son into th' adoption of the crown;
>
> (V.v.56)

but at the opening of the play it is presented simply as event. So is the jealousy of Leontes in *The Winter's Tale*. In the opening scene, two gentlemen, Camillo and Archidamus, intimates respectively of Leontes and Polixenes, congratulate themselves and each other on the long-continued rooted affection of the two kings; as Archidamus says, 'I think there is not in the world either malice or matter to alter it' (I.i.31). Almost at once we see that though there may not be matter, malice can burst through. For in spite of all that has been written in attempts to account for the jealousy of Leontes, it remains, like the anger of Cymbeline, finally inexplicable, welling up into an uncontrollable anguish unwarranted by anything that has happened. Leontes himself urges Hermione to press Polixenes to stay longer in Sicilia at the end of a visit that has lasted nine months in perfect amity and love. He leaps abruptly from the memory of her act of grace, in giving him her 'white hand' to seal their love, to the present contemplation of Hermione giving her hand in friendship to Polixenes; from satisfaction to the misery of 'tremor cordis' in the space of six lines or so:

> *Hermione*   But once before I spoke to th' purpose? when?
> Nay, let me have't; I long!
> *Leontes*   Why, that was when
> Three crabbed months had sour'd themselves to
>   death
> Ere I could make thee open thy white hand
> And clap thyself my love; then thou didst utter
> 'I am yours for ever'.
> *Hermione*   'Tis grace indeed,
> Why lo you now; I have spoke to th' purpose
>   twice:
> The one, for ever earn'd a royal husband;
> Th'other, for some while a friend.
> *Leontes*   [*Aside*] Too hot, too hot!
> To mingle friendship far, is mingling bloods.
> I have tremor cordis on me; my heart dances,
> But not for joy – not joy.
>
> (I.ii.100)

Hermione has been prettily trying to persuade Polixenes to stay, and Leontes congratulates her on her success; only once has she spoken to better purpose, in accepting him as husband. The transition from this to his initial blaze of jealousy is sudden; he turns aside to talk with Mamillius, as if to avoid the sight of Hermione and Polixenes together, but cannot help watching them, aware that he is acting as in a dream, a nightmare, but unable to stop what he calls 'the infection of my brains' (l. 145).

It is true that an actor playing Leontes could show incipient signs of passion before this point, but there is nothing in the text to warrant it. It seems rather that Shakespeare deliberately made Leontes blaze out unexpectedly in a concern precisely to leave aside or ignore questions of motive or possible explanations for his behaviour; the effect is to make us attend to the event, to accept what happens, and to take this change in Leontes as an unexplained incident in a dramatic world that may turn out to be full of strange happenings, a world like that of *Cymbeline*. There is no doubt about the violence of Leontes' jealousy as it emerges in the clotted and tortuous syntax of his speeches as Hermione and Polixenes go into the 'garden' (l. 178); and the substance of his lines reflects that 'infection' he feels, as if some disease suddenly strikes his imagination, corrupting his awareness of himself and others and making him act out a double role self-consciously as both fond husband and cuckold: so he sends Mamillius off,

> Go, play, boy, play; thy mother plays, and I
> Play too; but so disgrac'd a part, whose issue
> Will hiss me to my grave. . . .
>
> (I.ii.187)

The quibbles on the senses of 'play' (boy's play, amorous play, acting a part), and of 'disgrac'd' (ungraceful and shameful), show us Leontes, so to speak, consciously punning;[1] he is not, like Othello, absorbed by the passion he feels, but aware of it simultaneously as a role he is acting, and as a disease he thinks he can do nothing about, 'Physic for't there's none' (I.ii.200). This has the effect of distancing him and restricting the impact of his jealousy on the audience, for it does not well up out of his nature or 'character', but afflicts him from outside, as a sickness for which he is not responsible, and which, conceivably, might disappear as suddenly as it infected him.

Leontes is left on stage with Camillo, his familiar confidant and most trusted courtier, and, more than this, his confessor:

> I have trusted thee, Camillo,
> With all the nearest things to my heart, as well
> My chamber-counsels, wherein, priest-like, thou
> Hast cleans'd my bosom; I from thee departed
> Thy penitent reform'd.
>
> (I.ii.235)

Now, however, Leontes has changed his faith because of the infection of his mind, and Camillo cannot cleanse or reform him. At first Camillo cannot understand what Leontes is driving at, and when he realizes that Leontes thinks himself a

---

[1] These quibbles are finely analysed by M. M. Mahood in her *Shakespeare's Wordplay* (1957), pp. 149-50. See also *The Winter's Tale*, edited by J. H. P. Pafford (New Arden Shakespeare, 1963), p. 16.

cuckold, and Hermione guilty of adultery with Polixenes, he rejects the imputation as false, crying:

> Good my lord, be cur'd
> Of this diseas'd opinion, and betimes,
> For 'tis most dangerous.
>
> (I.ii.296)

No cure is to hand, and indeed, as Leontes goes on to claim rather that Hermione is infected, not he, Camillo gives every appearance of being persuaded. He has 'lov'd' Leontes (l. 324), who himself claims that the very outrageousness of his charges, and of his incitement to Camillo to poison Polixenes, gives them a kind of plausibility, and eventually he assents to the proposals of the King:

> I must believe you, sir;
> I do; and will fetch off Bohemia for't.
>
> (I.ii.333)

Now there comes another strange turn in the action, for, after pledging himself three times to take advantage of his office as cupbearer to Polixenes and poison him, he watches Leontes go off satisfied, and at once falls into a soliloquy in which he rejects his promise. When Polixenes enters, he tells him all, persuades him to leave the country, and arranges for them both to escape that night.

If this were a dramatic world in which the characters behaved in a psychologically realistic way, in accordance with their understanding of another's nature and motives, then we might expect Camillo to be a loyal servant, and try to help his master, as, for example, Kent does in *King Lear*. Instead, Camillo at first protests, but then goes along with Leontes and accepts the task of poisoning Polixenes, and finally runs away, simply abandoning the loved master who had brought him 'from meaner form . . . to worship' (l. 313). If his behaviour here is a little strange, so too is that of Polixenes in at once believing without question the testimony of Camillo against Leontes, and in rushing away from his lifelong friend with the main thought of saving his own skin, crying, 'Fear o'ershades me' (l. 457). The rooted affection of which we heard in the opening scene seems to evaporate in an instant, but the play ignores this; the

fact is that questions of loyalty or responsibility are not raised
here, and the characters are presented and behave as if not
fully in control of their actions. Like the gentleman in *Cymbeline*, they respond to events and to what others do with acceptance and wonder, rather than in terms of commitment or
judgment. Camillo sees that Leontes is infected, and by Polixenes,
who yet remains well, but cannot name or cure the disease:

> There is a sickness
> Which puts some of us in distemper, but
> I cannot name the disease, and it is caught
> Of you, that yet are well.

(I.ii.384)

They do not blame Leontes, but see him as sick, and themselves as liable to be afflicted by the 'distemper', which can
mean disease or derangement of the mind. Another image used
suggests that Leontes has been 'visited' in a different way, and
has suffered a kind of instantaneous conversion to a new religion;
so Camillo tells Polixenes:

> you may as well
> Forbid the sea for to obey the moon,
> As or by oath remove or counsel shake
> The fabric of his folly, whose foundation
> Is pil'd upon his faith, and will continue
> The standing of his body.

(I.ii.426)

Whether it is seen as a disease or as a settled faith, there is
nothing to be done about the rage of Leontes but to avoid it,
and so Camillo and Polixenes depart. We too are left to wonder
at what has happened, knowing that the world of this play holds
more strange things in store for us.

The flight of Camillo and Polixenes not only confirms Leontes
in his suspicion of Hermione, but makes his infection of the
mind range further, to the conviction that:

> There is a plot against my life, my crown;
> All's true that is mistrusted: that false villain
> Whom I employ'd was pre-employ'd by him,

(II.i.47)

In the rage of the disease, all that was 'mistrusted', all that
seemed impossible, is confirmed as true, and it becomes clear

I

to him that Hermione is about to bear not his child but Polixenes', though the length of his stay in Sicilia, nine months (I.ii.1), makes this barely possible. The denials of Hermione, and the protests of the lord and of Antigonus in II.i have no effect on him, and he stands alone, obsessed by a fantasy and convinced he is possessed of the truth. It is grotesque, and his speeches have a kind of shrillness, an incongruity with what we know to have happened, that brings them close to absurdity, as Antigonus himself points out for us when Leontes storms off to 'speak in public':

> Leontes   Come, follow us;
>   We are to speak in public; for this business
>   Will raise us all.
> Antigonus   [*Aside*] To laughter, as I take it,
>   If the good truth were known.
>
> (II.i.197)

We, the audience, know 'the good truth', and are simultaneously aware of Leontes as fantastic, as almost comic in the exaggerations of the delusions that possess him, and of the dire consequences produced by the 'dangerous, unsafe lunes i'th'king' (II.ii.30). His rage is at once absurd and, as Paulina calls it, a 'tyrannous passion' (II.iii.28), so that Leontes is distanced from us to the extent that we watch him acting out a kind of nightmare fantasy, even while his tyranny has a horrible immediacy for us.

The courtiers do their best to mitigate the effects of his affliction, but however much they may come, like Paulina, with

> words as medicinal as true,
> Honest, as either, to purge him of that humour
> That presses him from sleep,
>
> (II.iii.37)

they can do nothing. He calls Paulina a witch, and his reaction to the news of the birth of his daughter is to rage at the court as a 'nest of traitors', and to consign the babe as a bastard, Hermione as its mother, and Paulina herself as a witch, to the fire (II.iii.95, 113). Their attempts to moderate his fury bring one qualified success, when the spectacle of the entire court on their knees sways him to allow the babe to live. Even in this he carries out a mad 'justice' in requiring Antigonus, who with

Paulina has been mainly instrumental in saving the infant's life, on his oath to leave it in some 'desert place'; he says:

> As by strange fortune
> It came to us, I do in justice charge thee,
> On thy soul's peril and thy body's torture,
> That thou commend it strangely to some place
> Where chance may nurse or end it.
>
> (II.iii.178)

Leontes seems to mean 'foreign' by the word 'strange' here, and to be thinking of Polixenes, a 'stranger', whose child he believes it is; but we are aware of 'strange fortune' and 'chance' operating in a larger sense in the whole action. Mamillius has fallen ill just before Perdita is born, and the news of his death arrives just at the same time as the oracle from Delphos is delivered. Birth and death come together here, as they do a little later when Antigonus, having carried out his oath and left the babe on the imagined seacoast of Bohemia, is eaten by a bear. There is no sense in which Mamillius or Antigonus 'deserve' their deaths; the one is innocent, the other 'good'. Nor are their deaths lamented, but are treated rather as events that happen, and must be accepted, like the affliction of Leontes; no one is responsible for these things, which come unheralded, as the whims of fortune, strange yet true.

The death of Mamillius affects Hermione more than Leontes, and is mortal news to her, as Paulina says (III.ii.145); the report of her death follows hard on this. For Leontes the news of the death of Mamillius acts as an instantaneous cure of his infected mind, and his jealousy and rage disappear as quickly as they came. He moves in the space of five lines from a total rejection of the oracle as 'mere falsehood' (III.ii.138), to a crushing sense of his 'injustice' (l. 144). He is suddenly sane again, and recon‧ verted from his perverted faith to an understanding of his 'profaneness' against Apollo (l. 151). In all this Leontes is not condemned for his actions, or accused as though he were responsible for what he says and does. Paulina, Antigonus and the courtiers see clearly enough that he is wrong and tyrannous, but treat him as if he is mad, or ill with a disease they do not understand; Paulina professes herself his 'physician' (II.iii.54), but has no cure, only palliatives. What happens is unpredictable and inexplicable, and the characters accept things as they take place. At the same time, Leontes sends to Delphos for the oracle of Apollo in the hope that Hermione's guilt will be confirmed, and the oracle is accepted by all as a divine revelation. Leontes interprets the death of his son as a sign from Apollo that:

> the heavens themselves
> Do strike at my injustice,

(III.ii.143)

and is himself now afflicted with a sharp sense of guilt, which expresses itself in a determination to proclaim the goodness and 'piety' of Camillo. The report of Hermione's death moves him further to a sense that in some way he is responsible; he proposes that one grave shall hold her and Mamillius, and:

> upon them shall
> The causes of their death appear, unto
> Our shame perpetual.

(III.ii.233)

So although Leontes is not presented as being fully responsible for his words or deeds, but rather as diseased or mad, before the arrival of the oracle, he now sees himself as a man of sin, guilty of black deeds, and an offender against the gods. He accepts the authority of a divine order which only reveals itself in the oracle, and not in any obvious way in the ordinary affairs of life. Shakespeare contrives thus to have it both ways, and to make us aware of Leontes as not guilty, in so far as he seemed unable to help what he said and did before the arrival of the oracle, and yet plagued with a proper sense of guilt himself, inasmuch as he has offended. Yet he may still be widely wrong in his interpretation of the oracle; he sees the death of Mamillius as a punishment inflicted on himself, and the death of Hermione likewise, without considering whether these events might be interpretable as punishments inflicted on them. He proclaims Camillo a man of truth, mercy and piety, and yet we saw Camillo abandon Leontes and Hermione to flee with Polixenes; why did he not stay behind and attempt, like Paulina and Antigonus, to mitigate the effects of the King's jealous rage? In the next scene, Antigonus sees the storm that threatens his ship as expressing the anger of the heavens:

In my conscience,
The heavens with that we have in hand are angry,
And frown upon's.

(III.iii.4)

All the crew of the ship, and he, lose their lives, 'mocked' as
the clown says by the sea and the bear, and yet they are on an
errand of mercy, and in fact save the life of Perdita. These
things are not explicable in terms of motivation, cause and
consequence, deserved rewards or punishments, or responsibility. The heavens remain inscrutable, interfering in human
affairs unpredictably from time to time, in an oracle or a storm,
and then in such a way as to leave interpretation of the intervention ambiguous; to the immediate apprehension of the
characters and the audience, the world of the play seems
governed by chance and coincidence, and human nature itself,
as in the jealousy of Leontes, may change as unaccountably as
events do.

So when Hermione is suddenly faced with the charges of
Leontes that:

She's an adultress; I have said with whom:
More, she's a traitor,

(II.i.88)

her response to this just before she is carried off to prison is not
to blame him in any way, or think him responsible for this 'mistake' as she calls it, but simply to accept what is happening as a
kind of misfortune:

There's some ill planet reigns;
I must be patient till the heavens look
With an aspect more favourable.

(II.i.105)

Some malign influence from the heavens has caused her afflictions,
just as Perdita, 'haled out to murder', is 'starr'd most un-
luckily' (III.ii.97). At the same time, Hermione has a simple
confidence in her own innocence, and in the existence of 'powers
divine':

if powers divine
Behold our human actions (as they do),
I doubt not then but innocence shall make

False accusation blush, and tyranny
Tremble at patience.

(III.ii.26)

At her trial Hermione's patient stance in the face of horrible
accusations and threats, and her fearlessness in the face of
promised death ('life, I prize it not a straw', III.ii.107), reflect
her innocence and nobility; she has been associated with the
word 'grace' from early on (I.ii.76-105), as if to suggest in her
ideal of womanhood, and the trial scene fortifies this image of
her. But her disregard for life also appears as a right way of
reacting in a world so much subject to strange mischance,
sudden change, and the influence of ill planets. She knew as
she was taken off to prison and to endure her trial that:

this action I now go on
Is for my better grace.

(II.i.121)

The word 'grace' here may carry several meanings, but upper-
most seems to be the thought that what faces her will strengthen
her inwardly, by straining her patience and steadfastness, and
so reinforcing her humility in relation to an inscrutable providence. She must wait for the heavens to be more favourable.

The heavens, it seems, continue to look unfavourably, as
Paulina reports the death of Hermione, and the sorrows of
Leontes are complete in the loss of wife, son and daughter.
For the audience this is not all, since in the next scene Antigonus
and the crew of his ship are destroyed. Although Antigonus
feels himself to be 'most accurs'd' (III.iii.52) in carrying out his
oath and depositing the babe on a wild shore, we do not see him
as responsible; in the dream-vision he had the night before, he
reports how Hermione appeared to him, and spoke to him as
'Good Antigonus', without blaming him:

Since fate, against thy better disposition,
Hath made thy person for the thrower-out
Of my poor babe. . . .

(III.iii.28)

Fate now brings his death as another unexplained event in a
world of strange events. Mamillius and Hermione 'die' offstage,

but the visual image of the death of Antigonus is important both
as a climax to the sequence of disasters in the first part of the
play, and as an image to set against the recovery of the babe.
In order to make us focus on the event, to take our attention
from the character and prevent us from asking why Antigonus
is so picked on, Shakespeare provided an unusual, exciting and
most theatrical mode of dying for him. The bear draws all eyes,
including those of the Clown who watches and helps to guide
our response. The bear has provoked much discussion; some
think a real bear was used, some an actor, and some that it
was not seen but merely heard as noises off.[1] The dramatic
mode of the play, in my view, requires that the bear be played by
an actor whose antics are witnessed by the audience, and seen
as comic as well as savage. Antigonus dies a grotesque death,
in which the emphasis is all on the means of dying, so that, like
the shepherds, we are intrigued by the spectacle, and accept it
as an act of providence, a fact. Like them, we are made to take
things dying and things new-born with equal fortitude; nothing
surprises them in their world, where anything may happen, and
we too are made to feel that though the death of Antigonus is
sad, 'heavy matters', as the old Shepherd says, it is somehow
not very important, and not to be dwelt on.

Events then simply occur; it seems as if man's management
of affairs is at the mercy of chance and accident, and the
characters do not behave as if it lay in their wills to control
their lives. It is then, very appropriate that the Chorus at the
beginning of Act IV should be Time, who marks not only the
passage of sixteen years, but also the nature of this dramatic
world:

> I that please some, try all; both joy and terror
> Of good and bad, that makes and unfolds error,
> Now take upon me, in the name of Time,
> To use my wings. Impute it not a crime
> To me or my swift passage, that I slide
> O'er sixteen years, and leave the growth untried
> Of that wide gap, since it is in my power
> To o'erthrow law, and in one self-born hour

[1] This is in line with the interpretation of the bear offered by Nevil Coghill in
'Six Points of Stage-Craft in *The Winter's Tale*', *Shakespeare Survey*, 11 (1958),
pp. 34-5. Pafford, *op. cit.*, p. 69, like Dover Wilson, thinks a real bear was used.

To plant and o'erwhelm custom. Let me pass
The same I am, ere ancient'st order was,
Or what is now receiv'd.

Time might have appeared in many guises, as embodied in proverb, emblem and literary tradition, and it is tempting to associate him here with the idea of time as it appears elsewhere in the plays and poems of Shakespeare, or alternatively with the triumph of time as embodied, according to its subtitle, in Robert Greene's *Pandosto*, the principal source for the play. Time is commonly imaged either as *edax rerum*, time the destroyer, devouring time, or 'envious and calumniating time' in the phrases of Ulysses; or alternatively it appears as time the preserver, or vindicator of truth or virtue.[1] In *Pandosto*, the title-page informs us,[2]

is discovered by a pleasant History, that although by the means of sinister fortune Truth may be concealed, yet by Time, in spite of fortune, it is most manifestly revealed.

The narrative is much more concerned with fortune than with time, initially showing us inconstant Fortune turning her wheel to cover the 'sun of prosperity with the misty clouds of mishap and misery',[3] Fortune alternately revealing a friendly face, and turning to show a 'louring countenance';[4] but towards the end, fortune is brought into a general association with the gods, as when Dorastus (Florizel) curses 'the gods and fortune that they should cross him with such sinister chance'.[5] The title-page nevertheless indicates Greene's own idea of his tale, and Time does reveal the truth in spite of the mischances brought about by inconstant Fortune.

In many ways Shakespeare's play follows *Pandosto* closely,

---

[1] Inga-Stina Ewbank is, I think, mistaken in interpreting the play as 'The Triumph of Time in *The Winter's Tale*' (*Review of English Literature*, V (1964), 83-100, reprinted in *The Winter's Tale. A Collection of Critical Essays*, edited by Kenneth Muir, 1968, pp. 98-115), by analogy with the subtitle of its main source, *Pandosto*. She emphasizes Time the restorer, and thinks the action centring on Leontes is 'a dramatization of the failure to trust Time the Revealer' (p. 101); the restoration of Hermione she sees as 'a Triumph of Time' (p. 112). For a discussion of conventional images of Time, especially as preserver and destroyer see Erwin Panofsky, *Studies in Iconology* (1939; reissued 1962), pp. 81-4.
[2] Cited from Pafford's edition of *The Winter's Tale*, p. xxvii.
[3] *Ibid.*, p. 185.   [4] *Ibid.*, p. 202.   [5] *Ibid.*, p. 221.

but among the important differences must be included his treatment of fortune and of time. For the strange happenings and coincidences of *The Winter's Tale* are not seen as relating to fickle Fortune turning her wheel, but from the start appear rather as events connected somehow, in a way not understood by the characters, with the workings of an inscrutable providence. Time, as he appears with his hourglass and wings at the beginning of Act IV, proclaims himself to be both preserver and destroyer, but exists for us as something other than these functions. Time is here above all an observer; he brings joy and terror indifferently to good and bad, makes as well as unfolds error, and has the power to 'plant and o'erwhelm custom'. This figure of Time seems to claim his independence from human affairs, and his constancy even while he affects their fluctuations:

> The same I am, ere ancient'st order was,
> Or what is now receiv'd. I witness to
> The times that brought them in; so shall do
> To th' freshest things now reigning, and make stale
> The glistening of this present, as my tale
> Now seems to it.
>
> (IV.i.10)

Time is here the presenter of the action, separate from and a witness to the 'times' that change human order, and make stale the present. The play does not show the triumph of Time, who is not concerned to bring truth to light or vindicate innocence, but merely to present what happens; he is no moralizer or maker of patterns, but focuses our attention again on events, and if it is only through Time that the times as they change will disclose their meaning, then we must wait for the action to complete itself, for Time remains, like providence, inscrutable:

> let Time's news
> Be known when 'tis brought forth.
>
> (IV.i.26)

So we leap in imagination to Bohemia sixteen years later, where the lost child has grown into Perdita, who queens it at the shepherds' feast, and shows herself to be as cultivated as any princess should be. After storm and catastrophe, we pass to feast and song and dance, from a tale of winter to one of summer.

The sheep-shearing feast of IV.iv seems superficially to recover in action the image Polixenes had of himself and Leontes as boys:

> We were as twinn'd lambs that did frisk i'th'sun,
> And bleat the one at th'other: what we chang'd
> Was innocence for innocence; we knew not
> The doctrine of ill-doing, nor dream'd
> That any did.

(I.ii.67)

That golden image, however, belongs to memory, wish, or ideal, and the world of innocence as we see it is clouded in various ways, most immediately and obviously by the presence of the disguised Polixenes and Camillo, come to spy on the activities of Florizel. At first all is gaiety, but the scene progresses with an effect that may be compared to a masque in reverse. The celebrations begin with a dance 'of shepherds and shepherd-esses' (l. 165), in which Florizel and Perdita take the centre of attention, and she is the queen of the feast. After this dance, Autolycus arrives in the guise of a pedlar of knick-knacks and ballads, to provide songs and to remind us that 'there are cozeners abroad; therefore it behoves men to be wary' (l. 247). As Autolycus the rogue takes off the shepherdesses and the clown to make them 'pay well' for his trinkets, there enters a kind of antimasque of twelve men dressed as satyrs, 'men of hair', rough, wild, half-goat, whose presence seems to prompt Polixenes to reveal himself and separate Florizel from Perdita. Instead of the usual climax of a masque, in some form of beauty and virtue dispelling ugliness and evil, this masque-like sequence ends with the dance of goat-feet as anger and distress dispel gaiety and peace. Polixenes' blaze of anger is as sudden in effect as was the outburst of Leontes' jealousy at the opening of the play, and he seems to throw off his disguise to reveal not only the King, but a different man underneath. His wrath leads, like the jealousy of Leontes, to immediate threats of death and violence:

> *Polixenes*   Thou, old traitor,
> I am sorry that by hanging thee I can
> But shorten thy life one week. And thou, fresh piece

```
            Of excellent witchcraft, who, of force, must know
            The royal fool thou cop'st with –
Shepherd                              O, my heart!
Polixenes  I'll have thy beauty scratch'd with briers and made
            More homely than thy state.
                                              (IV.iv.412)
```

Florizel has offended, by offering, in the presence of Polixenes, to contract to marry Perdita without letting his father know, but this offence, to which Polixenes himself appears to be almost a party, for it is he who insists on hearing Florizel profess what he will do for his love, is not large enough to warrant the clamour Polixenes as King now raises. He threatens to hang the old shepherd, whose sole offence consists in being Perdita's apparent father, to destroy Perdita's beauty, and to bar Florizel from succession to the throne. It looks as though suffering and bitterness have returned, and the second half of the play may repeat in some sense the first, as the parallel is surely intended.

There are of course radical differences between the two parts of the play, as the last two acts have no deaths and are generally lighter in atmosphere. However, the 'innocent' world of the shepherds is darkened by more than the presence of Camillo and Polixenes, the entry of Autolycus, and the explosion of the King's anger. For it is here that disguise becomes a prominent feature of the play, as all the principal characters at the shepherd's festival are masked as something other than what they are. Polixenes and Camillo are disguised, presumably as old country-men and appear as acceptable guests at the feast; Autolycus appears in a new guise as a pedlar, having changed from the rags he was wearing in IV.iii. Perdita is pranked up as queen, 'no shepherdess' to Florizel, but 'Flora, Peering in April's front', a very goddess. In this garb, Perdita detects a change in herself, brought about by the fine robes she has on:

```
Methinks I play as I have seen them do
In Whitsun pastorals; sure this robe of mine
Does change my disposition.
                                              (IV.iv.133)
```

As she, 'goddess-like prank'd up' (l. 10), discovers that in her finery she can act like a queen, so Florizel, who is in disguise as the shepherd Doricles, seems to her 'vilely bound up' (l. 22), and in the clothes of baseness becomes base indeed to the extent that he attempts to deceive and disobey his father. This use of disguise has links with the famous interchange between Polixenes and Perdita on nature and art, which has been emphasized to the neglect of other important matters in thematic treatments of the play. Perdita speaks in her distaste for carnations, or 'nature's bastards' as she calls them, as if there is some unnatural art in their creation; and Polixenes retorts to the effect that 'any man-made means of improving nature is itself the creation of nature, since man and his powers are also natural':[1]

> so, over that art,
> Which you say adds to nature, is an art
> That nature makes. You see, sweet maid, we marry
> A gentler scion to the wildest stock,
> And make conceive a bark of baser kind
> But bud of nobler race. This is an art
> Which does mend nature – change it rather – but
> The art itself is nature.

(IV.iv.90)

The irony in these words of Polixenes, who is about to prevent in anger the marriage of his own son to a wild stock has been much noticed; but there is a deeper irony in the whole interchange as it relates to disguise. Perdita, 'poor lowly maid' (l. 9), is transformed by her robes into a queen and feels her disposition change; here might Polixenes see art mending nature, if he were to apply his words, and the art revealing itself as nature, for Perdita is in fact a princess. Polixenes, also in disguise, has changed nature to appear as a simple and gentle old man, which is perhaps to 'mend nature' if his real self appears only when he throws off his disguise to vent his anger on Florizel, Perdita and the Shepherd.

Having made his angry threats, Polixenes leaves the stage, and Florizel determines to defy his father and put his oath to Perdita above his duty. Camillo is there to arrange the business for him, less in service to him than in order to satisfy his own desire to see his home in Sicily again:

[1] Citing Pafford's note on this passage in his New Arden edition of the play, p. 93.

His going I could frame to serve my turn,
Save him from danger, do him love and honour,
Purchase the sight again of dear Sicilia
And that unhappy king my master, whom
I so much thirst to see.

(IV.iv.501)

Camillo abandoned one master, Leontes, in Act I, and now is disloyal to a second, Polixenes; but he stage-manages the affair so well that it seems 'almost a miracle' (l. 526) to Florizel, as Camillo imagines for him the voyage he proposes to Sicily, and the kindest of welcomes Florizel and Perdita will receive from Leontes. It seems that at some point, perhaps after his father's exit, Florizel has removed the smock in which he appeared a 'poor humble swain' (l. 30), to appear in state as prince, for now it becomes necessary for him and Perdita to disguise themselves afresh, on Camillo's advice, in order to reach shipboard safely. So Florizel exchanges garments with Autolycus, who happens along conveniently, and Perdita does her best to act a new role:

> take your sweetheart's hat
> And pluck it o'er your brows, muffle your face,
> Dismantle you, and (as you can) disliken
> The truth of your own seeming; that you may
> (For I do fear eyes over) to shipboard
> Get undescried.
> *Perdita*   I see the play so lies
> That I must bear a part.

(IV.iv.640)

Perdita must disliken or disguise the truth of her seeming or appearance; she has appeared a goddess or queen, but knows herself to be a 'poor lowly maid', a shepherd's daughter; while we know a deeper truth still, that she is in fact a princess, now putting on another seeming as she takes Florizel's hat, and muffles her face. It is to take part in Camillo's play, and yet the role may in some sense represent the person, as Autolycus gives us a different perspective on what we see:

> The prince himself is about a piece of iniquity (stealing away from his father with his clog at his heels): if I thought it were a piece of honesty to acquaint the king withal, I would not

do't; I hold it the more knavery to conceal it; and therein am
I constant to my profession.

(IV.iv.665)

If it would be a piece of honesty for Autolycus to inform
Polixenes, it is not so for Camillo, who plans to develop the
action of his little play by telling the king:

> Of this escape and whither they are bound;
> Wherein my hope is I shall so prevail
> To force him after.

(IV.iv.652)

In doing this he takes a risk, and betrays Florizel. Meanwhile
Autolycus, dressed in the courtier's clothes given to him by
Florizel, encounters the Shepherd and his son, and, upon
removing the beard he wore as pedlar ('let me pocket up my
pedlar's excrement', he says, taking it off on stage, l. 703), he is
at once taken by the rustics for a courtier on his own claim:

> *Shepherd*   Are you a courtier, and't like you, sir?
> *Autolycus*   Whether it like me or no, I am a courtier.
> Seest thou not the air of the court in these enfold-
> ings? hath not my gait in it the measure of the
> court? receives not thy nose court-odour from me?
> Reflect I not on thy baseness, court-contempt? . . .

(IV.iv.717)

The Shepherd and his son accept him as what he seems to be,
and since they need an advocate at court to present the package
that will identify Perdita, Autolycus believes he has found in
them a means of restoring his fortunes. Later on, when the
Shepherd and Clown have been received at court, welcomed
as the saviours of Perdita, and in turn put on court clothes, they
too become instant courtiers, and can lord it over Autolycus:

> *Clown*   You are well met, sir. You denied to fight with me
> the other day, because I was no gentleman born.
> See you these clothes? Say you see them not and
> think me still no gentleman born: you were best
> say these robes are not gentleman born. Give me the
> lie, do, and try whether I am not now a gentleman
> born.
> *Autolycus*   I know you are now, sir, a gentleman born.

(V.ii.124)

In these very funny scenes, we enjoy the cleverness of the trickster Autolycus, and the way in which the simplicity of the Clown shows through his new finery. Yet they are changed too, even though in some sense they remain the same; clothes seem to make the man, and art in this way conceals, alters, sometimes mends nature. These disguises belong with a series of 'transformations', to use Florizel's word in talking about the shape he puts on to woo Perdita (IV.iv.31), which culminate in the restoration to life of the 'statue' Hermione. They also indicate various possibilities for deceit and sharp practice. It is, after all, only because of Camillo's ingenuity that Florizel sails to his father, and not, as he intended, away from Polixenes; Autolycus deceiving the peasants is matched by Florizel deceiving his father, and Camillo tricking both Florizel and Polixenes. The final reconciliation between Florizel and his father through the mediation of Leontes was not intended by either of them.

It is a partial view of the last two acts of the play that sees in them only sweetness and light, pastoral peace and gaiety, and it would be equally a partial view that finds only a pattern of lies and deceptions, and of art affecting nature for the worse, as if to elaborate on Perdita's mistrust of the effect of art on nature. Both perspectives are, however, important, and the second has not received much attention. The second half of the play, unlike the first part, has both a Clown, the only title given to the Shepherd's son, and a fool, in so far as Autolycus, by virtue of being out of service, a kind of outcast, can act in part as a witty hanger-on and mocker of others. At the same time, Autolycus is firmly and strongly shown to be a rogue, a natural and incorrigible thief, liar and cheat. This is worth emphasizing, because he has often been seen as 'a blend of burly comedian and lyrical jester',[1] or as a figure introduced to 'keep the earthly paradise sufficiently earthly without disturbing the paradisiac state';[2] alternatively;[3]

[1] G. Wilson Knight, *The Crown of Life* (1947), p. 100.
[2] E. M. W. Tillyard, *Shakespeare's Last Plays* (1938), quoted in *Shakespeare; 'The Winter's Tale'*, edited Kenneth Muir, p. 86.
[3] Charles R. Crow, 'Chiding the Plays: Then till now', *Shakespeare Survey*, 18 (1965), p. 8. In the following year J. R. Brown published his essay 'Laughter in the last plays' (in *Later Shakespeare*, Stratford-upon-Avon Studies, 8, edited J. R. Brown and Bernard Harris, 1966, pp. 103-25; it is reprinted with slight revisions in *Shakespeare's Plays in Performance*, 1966, pp. 91-112), in which he

there has been silence about him. Traversi, in the shorter
of his two examinations of the play, makes not a single
reference to Autolycus in the twenty-three pages of the
chapter. . . . With other critics the silence is not quite absolute,
but Autolycus gets a barest minimum of their attention. Van
Doren's chapter on the play has one reference: 'the surpassing
roguery of Autolycus'. Baldwin Maxwell, in an introduction to
the play that runs to eight pages, has two references . . .
Frank Kermode, also in an introduction, this one running to
fifteen pages, mentions Autolycus once, and in parentheses.
What he says is significant: 'The mood [of Act IV] is of innocence (even Autolycus contributes to this, partly by
establishing rustic virtues as opposed to those of the court –
an old pastoral theme, and one paralleled by the debates
between Touchstone and Corin in *As You Like It*) . . .'
Here Autolycus is not seen or cherished as a character 'strongly
represented' [in Dr Johnson's words] but as a contributor
to the theme that Kermode names . . . These critics, all of
them except Johnson, find the serious movement of the play
to be remarkably significant without Autolycus.

This may be overstating the case, but it would seem reasonable
to ask that an explanation of the role of Autolycus should be
an essential part of any account of the play, and many of those
who praise him find little reason for his presence. It is worth
stressing, therefore, the extent to which his roguery is substantial; if he does no real harm, it is not altogether for want of
trying. He stands out as a 'real' figure in this artificial romance-
world of Bohemia, and in spite of 'his classical name, Autolycus
is an English coney-catcher',[1] making an especially strong

---

argues that the role of Autolycus 'must be a clown's star performance, or nothing'
(p. 116), and explains his presence in the play thus: 'In an intensely felt narrative,
he evokes from the audience laughter, connivance and appreciation, relaxation
and admiration. In a drama about the influences of time, he provides a timeless
artistry and remains unchanged at the conclusion. He brings topicality to a
fantastic tale, an escape from the consequences of knavery to a moral confrontation, and a grotesque embodiment of irresponsible fears and aggressions, of
vigorous and sexual activity, to a shapely and often refined romance' (p. 118).
This is by far the best account of Autolycus I know, but I think overstresses his
'star' role in providing 'irresponsible enjoyment'. Played in this way, Autolycus
unbalances the last part of the play by drawing all attention to himself, as he was
allowed to do in the 1969 Royal Shakespeare Company production; and it was
for something more than irresponsibility that he was whipped from court.
[1] M. M. Mahood, *Shakespeare's Wordplay*, p. 157.

impact in the theatre. Although his natural rascality is softened by his songs and gaiety, it represents a genuine element of subversion; he is a disgraced courtier, whose business is to steal, to defraud, to rejoice when he can cry, 'What a fool Honesty is! and Trust, his sworn brother, a very simple gentleman!', and congratulate himself upon having 'picked and cut most of their festival purses' (IV.iv.587ff.). Although it happens that his schemes may go awry, it is his ingrained habit to be corrupt, and to corrupt others. When we last see him, he is about such a business, ingratiating himself with the Shepherd and Clown now they are turned courtiers, and flattering them in the hope of serving his own ends. Autolycus has sometimes been compared with Falstaff, and they have some characteristics in common,[1] but there is this important difference, that Falstaff is in the end rejected by Hal and sent to prison for correction, whereas Autolycus seems about to recover his place at court, as he persuades the Clown to lie on his behalf:

> Clown   If it be ne'er so false, a true gentleman may swear
>   it in the behalf of his friend; and I'll swear to the
>   prince thou art a tall fellow of thy hands and that
>   thou wilt not be drunk; but I know thou art no tall
>   fellow of thy hands and that thou wilt be drunk;
>   but I'll swear it, and I would thou wouldst be a tall
>   fellow of thy hands.
> Autolycus I will prove so, sir, to my power.
>
> (V.ii.156)

The Shepherd and Clown promise to be his 'good masters', and as simple honesty is visibly changing here to court hypocrisy, and a true gentleman may swear to any falsehood, they may reinstate him with 'the princes, our kindred'. So, we may suppose, life will proceed, bringing more corruption as well as more joy, more suffering as well as more recoveries and reconciliations that seem almost miracles, while Time unfolds, 'both joy and terror Of good and bad'.

Autolycus helps to focus the differences between the first three acts and the last two. He is the one figure in the play who sleeps out the thought of 'the life to come' (IV.iii.28) in the happy exercise of those vices for which he was whipped from

---

[1] As, for instance, by G. Wilson Knight in *The Crown of Life*, pp. 100, 112.

K

court. He is naturally addicted to the deceptions and disguises which others in Bohemia adopt for special purposes; but these others, Florizel, Camillo, Polixenes, even Perdita, are linked with him in practising arts which are natural to him, and if to him perhaps to humanity – arts not in themselves good, and closely allied to vice. Autolycus remains an enjoyable figure because he lacks malice, which is to say that he does not so much seek to do harm to others, as to accept what fortune throws in his way; he is indeed what he calls himself on his first appearance, a 'snapper-up of unconsidered trifles' (IV.iii.26), a cozener of the fools who happen to cross his path. A character who in some ways parallels Autolycus is Camillo, who manipulates the affairs of Polixenes and Florizel as Autolycus works on the Shepherd and his son the Clown. Camillo tricks and deceives others, but escapes censure partly because the end, a harmony which includes the restoration of Hermione, transcends the means he uses, and partly because everyone has such confidence in him as 'good Camillo'.[1] We are also aware of him as presenter of the action involving Florizel and the King, as he manages his own play, deciding on the roles the prince and Perdita will play, and arranging for their welcome by Leontes:

> It shall be so my care
> To have you royally appointed, as if
> The scene you play were mine.

>> (IV.iv.583)

In this aspect he seems almost a preliminary sketch for Prospero, but remains something less than a controller of people and events; as Autolycus relies on Fortune to drop booties in his mouth, so Camillo puts his trust in the 'hope' that his plans may prevail (IV.iv.654). Camillo and Autolycus may be managers of affairs, but only to a limited degree, and both rely on chance or fortune, as is symbolized in the sea-journeys undertaken by Florizel and Perdita, and then by Camillo and Polixenes, which parallel the journeys of Antigonus and Perdita on the one hand, and of Camillo and Polixenes on the other

---

[1] He is so called at ll. 505 and 571, and is 'worthy' at l. 546, in Florizel's address. Polixenes had called him 'good Camillo', and 'my best Camillo' (IV.ii.1, 51). See also the references to his honesty by Hermione (III.ii.72), and to his goodness by Leontes (III.ii.153, 159).

hand, in the first part of the play; for may not another storm blow up, such as the one that destroyed the ship of Antigonus? That sense of a world where anything may happen, and all events must be referred to fortune or chance for immediate understanding and acceptance, and only then to a possible remote and inscrutable providence, thus continues to some extent through both parts of the action. The difference in the second part is that the attempts by Camillo and Autolycus to interfere in and manage the affairs of others convey the sense of a beneficent outcome, as Camillo's intrigues work out with evident success, and the Fortune to which Autolycus appeals is palpably making him the agent for bringing to light the secret of Perdita's birth. The sense of a providence overseeing all, of the heavens looking at last with a favourable aspect, is brought sharply to our awareness here in the way in which fortune aids Camillo and deceives Autolycus, that is, in the extent to which they seem to be in the event managing others only in fulfilment of larger purposes they do not comprehend.

A sense of wonder still prevails among the characters, as is brought out in the reports in V.ii of Leontes discovering Perdita to be his daughter, and of the reconciliation between the kings, and between them and Florizel, Shakespeare does not show these things in action, presumably to reserve his final grand dramatic effect for the restoration of Hermione; by having them reported he also neatly avoids any possibilities latent in the situation of recriminations, and is enabled to emphasize how the discoveries seem 'so like an old tale that the verity of it is in strong suspicion' (V.ii.28). Leontes and Polixenes can hardly credit what they hear, which is 'like an old tale still' (l. 59), and a 'notable passion of wonder' (l. 14) appears in them as an appropriate reaction to the unexpected and extraordinary revelations they hear, as ancient quarrels dissolve and the lost child is recovered. The audience has lived through these events, and looks on as the gentlemen describe the 'very notes of admiration' (l. 11) the report of them produces at court. The last scene of the play, however, brings a revelation that is as unexpected to the audience as it is to Leontes, in the coming to life of the statue of Hermione, and the audience is brought in to share the 'amazement' of the characters at another strange and almost, it seems, miraculous event, which:

Were it but told you, should be hooted at
Like an old tale.

(V.iii.116)

Wonder here is almost transformed into faith, indeed is so, momentarily, for Leontes, as Paulina calls on him to awake his faith, and stages a resurrection as if Leontes is giving her life and redeeming her; she calls to the 'statue':

Bequeath to death your numbness; for from him
Dear life redeems you.

(V.iii.102)

A scene suggestive of masque is transformed almost into ritual, or magic, as music makes the 'statue', standing as an image in a 'chapel' (l. 86), goddess-like, come to life. As Perdita appeared to Florizel like Flora, a queen among the petty gods, so now Hermione seems a goddess, and is approached with a kind of religious awe by Leontes, as Paulina says to him:

Start not; her actions shall be holy as
You hear my spell is lawful.

(V.iii.104)

Hermione, who earlier had been so conscious of 'grace', seems to become now a living emblem of grace and restitution. Hermione moves to speak to her daughter, not to Leontes; words between them are unnecessary, for what matters is the act of faith on his part, committing himself again to her as a living woman. So it seems at last to Leontes that the series of strange events is brought to a completion, and that the gods show their hand in it, as Florizel and Perdita came together and are betrothed, the 'heavens directing' (V.iii.150).

If there is pattern, it is seen only in retrospect, and in any case cannot be complete; the betrothal of the young prince and princess is part of a continuing sequence of events to be unfolded by Time. The coming to life of Hermione is also a great dramatic gesture, for the moment crushing doubts and speculations, and showing the heavens looking with an aspect more favourable than at the beginning of the play, but the pressure of the action as a whole is to place this as the last in a series of strange happenings under an uncertain providence which destroys Mamillius and Antigonus, while preserving Perdita and

Hermione, and under which human beings grope in affliction, error, in good fortune and bad fortune, through time, not knowing what it will bring next. If the end of the play is optimistic, it is also clear-sighted, as is reflected also in a third way in which we are invited to respond to the statue-scene. For in this Paulina takes over as 'presenter' of a masque or playlet she has contrived. In the first three acts, Leontes, afflicted by madness, disease or some perverted faith as others see him, stages, so to speak, a dreadful farce, absurd and appropriate for laughter, as Antigonus suggests (II.i.198), but terrifying too, as it leads to the death of Antigonus, the apparent death of Hermione, and the loss of Perdita. In Act IV Camillo takes over as the much more conscious presenter of the action, arranging for Florizel and Polixenes both to sail to Sicily, and providing parts, and costumes even, as when he persuades Perdita to take on her role, and she disguises herself, saying:

> I see the play so lies
> That I must bear a part

(IV.iv.645)

Autolycus also stages his private actions in this part of the play, and in the last scene Paulina takes over from all these. In the statue of Hermione, we are told by a gentleman in V.ii, Julio Romano has created a figure so like nature that one might 'speak to her and stand in hope of answer' (V.ii.97). In fact, Paulina's art goes beyond that of Julio Romano, to become 'magic' (V.iii.39, 110), in making the statue live. It is a noble art to recover nature so, but we also see it as the outcome of a long deception practised on Leontes by Paulina and Hermione, and as a little masque-like drama within the play. Perdita distrusts art, as it appears from her conversation with Polixenes in IV.iv, when it seems to compete with or do the work of nature, and her fastidiousness is borne out in so far as the play shows art as, at one end of the spectrum, artifice, trickery, deception, disguise, cheating. Polixenes replies with a recognition that art and nature cannot be so easily separated, though he applies this narrowly and ironically in relation to Florizel, only in terms of grafting. The play applies the general point more extensively, showing us how art, at the other end of the spectrum of its significances, may indeed mend nature, how deception and disguise may be used to bring about restoration and harmony, how art includes all the skills of civilization, rising to their highest in those religious or magical arts conducted by the priests who mediate the oracle of Apollo, and by Paulina enacting her ritual in the chapel at the end. The bringing to life of Hermione focuses the contradictions in the relation of art to nature; here art and nature come together beneficially, and with a sense of miracle, and yet Paulina is also stage-managing the climax to the grossest piece of trickery in the play. The scene holds the paradoxes in suspension, for they cannot be resolved. Perdita, who rejects artifice, yet disguises herself, pretending to be Flora; it is natural to practise art, and art involves artifice, the deliberate desire to deceive which can emerge as vice in Autolycus. Perhaps the nicest touch at the end of the play occurs when Leontes takes over as stage manager in his final speech, and thrusts together in marriage those inveterate artists and contrivers, Camillo and Paulina; they lead off the company, at the request of Leontes, for a review of the roles they have all been playing:

> Good Paulina,
> Lead us from hence, where we may leisurely
> Each one demand, and answer to his part
> Perform'd in this wide gap of time, since first
> We were dissever'd: hastily lead away.

(V.iii.151)

(iv) *The Tempest*

Although *The Tempest* has much in common with *Cymbeline* and *The Winter's Tale,* and has often been interpreted as a kind of 'necessary development' from them, it is also in many ways a new departure as a play. Thematic resemblances between these plays have been charted, and they have been analysed as different versions of the same basic 'myth';[1] but however they may be linked in these ways, *The Tempest* has its own distinctive structure, sets up its own peculiar pattern of expectations, and demands to be assessed as a unique work of art in its own

[1] See, for example, G. Wilson Knight, *The Shakespearian Tempest* (1932), and *The Crown of Life* (1947); also D. A. Traversi, *Shakespeare; The Last Phase* (1954), and Frank Kermode's discussion of critical attitudes to the play in his Introduction to the New Arden edition (1958), pp. lxxxiv-lxxxv.

right. Some of the more obvious peculiarities of this play would seem at first sight to set it apart from the others. Instead of an inscrutable providence manifesting itself from time to time in oracles, miracles, or appearances of gods, this play has in Prospero a controller who exercises through his magic a power like that of heaven. Certain oppositions in it, such as those between beauty and ugliness, or nurture (education) and nature (brutishness) seem so schematically rendered, as in the contrasts between Caliban and Miranda, as to allow an allegorical inter-pretation.[1] The extensive use of masque and spectacle has also encouraged a treatment of the whole play as based on masque.[2] At the same time, *The Tempest* is the only one among the late plays that observes the neo-classical unities of time and place. All these features in themselves suggest that Shakespeare was moving in a new direction in this play, a view confirmed by an examination of its dramatic shaping.

At the beginning of I.ii, Miranda confirms our impression of what we have witnessed in the opening scene, a shipwreck in which all, boat and crew alike, were lost; she suffered with those she saw suffer, watched the ship 'Dash'd all to pieces' (l. 8), and is convinced the people on it died, 'Poor souls, they perish'd!' (l. 9). She is amazed (l. 14), but accepts what has happened, supposing her father may have raised the storm by his art, but not that he has caused the wreck. In fact she and we quickly learn that he has ordered the shipwreck, but:

> I have with such provision in mine Art
> So safely ordered, that there is no soul –
> No, not so much perdition as an hair
> Betid to any creature in the vessel
> Which thou heard'st cry, which thou saw'st sink.

(I.ii.28)

---

[1] On the question of allegory in relation to the play, see A. D. Nuttall, *Two Concepts of Allegory* (1967). *The Tempest* is also sometimes treated as if it were to be properly regarded less as play than as poem; so Reuben Brower calls it 'a Metaphysical poem of metamorphosis' in his essay, 'The Mirror of Analogy', included in his book, *The Fields of Light* (1951), and reprinted in *Shakespeare: 'The Tempest'*, edited D. J. Palmer (1968), pp. 153-75.

[2] See Enid Welsford's *The Court Masque* (1927), pp. 336-49; the climax of the play for her lay in the discovery of Ferdinand and Miranda playing chess, and she wrote, 'the spirit of *The Tempest* is far nearer to the spirit of masque than is *Comus*' (p. 340).

What we saw happened, and yet did not happen; Prospero's art is so powerful that with his 'provision' or foresight (supposing this word to be a correct emendation of the Folio reading 'compassion'), he can destroy and save simultaneously.[1] He has, through the agency of Ariel, dispersed the crew in groups about the island, and the ship, as we learn when the boatswain returns in V.i. is undamaged. If what he has done on one level is to deceive by a trick or illusion, some vanity of his art, on another level what he has done is real, as it controls the actions of people, and shapes the course of events.

At the same time Prospero's art is limited, and in narrating to Miranda the history of Antonio's usurpation of Milan, and of the way in which she and her father were left to drift at sea in a 'rotten carcass of a butt' (l. 146), Prospero also indicates something of what the nature and limits of his art are. For one thing, his magic powers seem to have been acquired since he and Miranda arrived on Setebos, for he was unable to foresee or prevent Antonio and Sebastian depriving him of his dukedom, and counter their treachery. Moreover, these powers are in some sense a function of the island, and only operate in its vicinity. Their development has to do with the books which Gonzalo provided for Prospero, 'volumes that I prize above my dukedom' (l. 167), and with the latter's 'secret studies' (l. 77) when he was in Milan; their nature perhaps is connected with that neglect of worldly ends for the bettering of his mind Prospero speaks of, with the sense we have of his goodness. Human treachery drove him from Milan, and he was saved, he tells Miranda, 'By Providence divine' (l. 159); now a strange chance has brought his enemies to the island:

> By accident most strange, bountiful Fortune,
> (Now my dear lady) hath mine enemies
> Brought to this shore; and by my prescience
> I find my zenith doth depend upon
> A most auspicious star, whose influence
> If now I court not, but omit, my fortunes
> Will ever after droop.

(I.ii.178)

---

[1] For other instances of Prospero's ability to foresee what is to happen, see I.ii.180 and II.i.288.

Fortune, once hostile to him, brought about his fall, but is now his 'dear lady', and he must seize the opportunity she offers. So Prospero's powers are circumscribed, dependent geographically on the island, and operating in relation to providence on the one hand, and fortune on the other.

The zenith or highest point of Prospero's fortunes will in any case be to recover what he has lost, and reinstate himself as:

> the Duke of Milan, and
> A prince of power.
>
> (I.ii.54)

His magical art or power subserves another end, that of regaining his temporal or princely power; and it is with this in mind that he has educated Miranda carefully as a princess (l. 172). Indeed, he has made himself ruler of the strange island, and by his magic art has made Ariel and Caliban his servants, or rather, to use his own word, his slaves. Ariel had been imprisoned within a cloven pine by the witch Sycorax until Prospero released him; he had been 'her servant' and has now become Prospero's, earning his eventual liberty through service. Prospero requires absolute obedience, and no complaint:

> If thou more murmur'st, I will rend an oak
> And peg thee in his knotty entrails, till
> Thou hast howl'd away twelve winters.
>
> (I.ii.294)

The threatened punishment coincides exactly in nature and length of time with that inflicted on Ariel by Sycorax, which was, as Prospero describes it, 'a torment To lay upon the damn'd' (l. 289). So although Ariel and Prospero respect each other as 'great master' (l. 189), and 'Fine apparition! My quaint Ariel' (l. 317), their relationship is basically that of slave and master. Prospero's other slave, Caliban, serves him and Miranda in the most menial offices, and is despised by Miranda as a 'villain', and by Prospero as a 'poisonous slave' (ll. 309, 319); he is imprisoned in a 'hard rock' (l. 343) by his own and Miranda's account, hates his service and his master and mistress, and for the slightest sign of unwillingness in carrying out commands, he is racked with horrible pains and tortures. Miranda tried to educate him, and taught him language as Prospero had taught her, but the purposes of his brutish nature could only seem vile to her, as he would not take 'any print of goodness' (l. 352); his imprisonment and slavery are apparently punishments for his 'wickedness' in seeking to rape Miranda. The standards Prospero applies are those of Milan, of his own civilization, and Caliban's version of what has happened raises some questions about the validity of those standards on the isle. For Prospero is himself in some sense a usurper, as he has taken the island from Caliban, who in the first place 'educated' him by showing him 'all the qualities o'th'isle' (l. 337), and who now can lament with some reason;

> I am all the subjects that you have,
> Which first was mine own king,
>
> (I.ii.341)

After the shipwreck of the opening scene, Prospero's first exercise of his art is to use Ariel to lure Ferdinand to the presence of Miranda. At the first glance they see one another as 'thing divine' (l. 418) and 'goddess' (l. 421), but know themselves for man and woman too, and duly fall in love, as Prospero desires; how far his art has effected this is not clear, but for them to be in love is to put them 'both in either's powers' (l. 450). Ferdinand has entered half in grief, and weeping the King his father's death, and half in self-congratulation, as now he can say, 'myself am Naples' (l. 434); but here he is in Prospero's kingdom, and in his power, as, like Jupiter 'crossing' Posthumus in *Cymbeline*, Prospero makes Ferdinand suffer:

> thou dost here usurp
> The name thou ow'st not; and hast put thyself
> Upon this island as a spy, to win it
> From me, the lord on't.
>
> *Ferdinand*　　　　　　No, as I am a man.
> *Miranda*　There's nothing ill can dwell in such a temple:
> If the ill spirit have so fair a house,
> Good things will strive to dwell with't.
> *Prospero*　　　　　　Follow me.
> Speak not you for him: he's a traitor. Come;
> I'll manacle thy neck and feet together. . . .
>
> (I.ii.453)

Prospero imposes on Ferdinand tasks fit for a slave, and, in the same sense that it applied earlier to Caliban, 'imprisons' him;

this is designed as a kind of test, or rather, education in self-rule, and the presence of Miranda makes confinement easy; so Ferdinand cries:

> all corners else o'th'earth
> Let liberty make use of; space enough
> Have I in such a prison.
>
> (I.ii.491)

At the same time, we witness a display of power by Ferdinand's 'enemy' (l. 466), Prospero, who speaks as if he were King indeed, twice using the word 'traitor', which rings somewhat oddly on the island; it is also in its way an exercise of tyranny, and the 'punishment' Ferdinand has to endure corresponds exactly to that inflicted upon Caliban, who had attempted to violate Miranda. In II.ii Caliban enters carrying wood, and meets Trinculo and Stephano, whose wine makes him drunk, frees him from Prospero's impositions, and enables him to escape to the forbidden parts of the island. Ferdinand in effect takes the place of Caliban, and the following scene (III.i) opens with him 'bearing a log'.

Prospero rules as King, and uses his magic arts to order his kingdom somewhat as if it were still Milan, as when he uses a term like 'traitor'. He has in some sense usurped upon Caliban's island, and imprisoned him; but in another perspective, Prospero himself has seen his own kingdom usurped, and is himself 'imprisoned' on an uncivilized island. Here what Prospero has learned by the necessary exercise of patience and self-rule will emerge in the course of the play, as will the way the harshness he imposes matches the harshness he has suffered. He is also a father carefully arranging an appropriate marriage for his daughter, but delighted, too, to find that she and Ferdinand at once fall in love – delighted and at the same time angry:

Miranda   Sir, have pity;
    I'll be his surety.
Prospero   Silence! one word more
    Shall make me chide thee, if not hate thee. What!
    An advocate for an impostor!

> (I.ii.475)

Prospero says he must make their courtship difficult, 'lest too light winning Make the prize light' (l. 451), but they do not know this, and to them he is simply cross-grained and harsh. He becomes temporarily, and in a minor perspective, a father-figure out of conventional romantic comedy, opposing his daughter's wishes, because the fulfilment of her desires will end parental control over her. The lovers are now in the power of each other, and through this gain a kind of freedom, just as Caliban gains a different kind of freedom when drunk. So in III.i, Miranda, watching Ferdinand bearing logs, promises to be his 'servant' (l. 85), even as he accepts the 'bondage' of love to become her 'slave': *— love associated with imprisonment.*

> The very instant that I saw you, did
> My heart fly to your service; there resides,
> To make me slave to it; and for your sake
> Am I this patient log-man.
>
> (III.i.64)

Prospero may impose bodily labour on Ferdinand, but the power of love is greater than Prospero's in the sense that it transmutes menial slavery into service to Miranda, and makes Ferdinand's labours into pleasures.

Meanwhile, Alonso, cast up on the island with his little 'court' remains inconsolable in the conviction that his son and heir, Ferdinand, has drowned. The good Gonzalo likewise wrongly assumes that Ferdinand is dead, and, in his attempts to comfort the King, gets his facts wrong about the location of Tunis, and proposes such a self-contradictory idea of a commonwealth that he lays himself open to the mockery of Sebastian and Antonio. In all this he 'talks nothing' (II.i.164) to Alonso to encourage 'merry fooling' (l. 168) and relieve the mood of the King. Gonzalo's image of the ideal commonwealth he would establish if he could colonize the isle and 'were the King on't' (l. 139) may in some sense be a critique of the primitivism of the essay of Montaigne on which it is largely based, but in any case it has an immediate and potent relevance to the action of the play. His ideal commonwealth would have no laws, no magistrates, no contracts, no inheritance, no letters, no labour and no treason or crime:

No occupation; all men idle, all;
And women too, but innocent and pure:
No sovereignty. . . .

(II.i.148)

It would be a return to a prelapsarian Eden, with Nature bringing forth of itself all necessities, but an Eden filled with his
'innocent people' (l. 158); and yet Gonzalo would be king:

I would with such perfection govern, sir,
T'excel the Golden Age.

(II.i.161)

A people of such innocence would not need to be governed, but
a king might well wish to have a state such as Gonzalo imagines.
Gonzalo talked 'nothing', but something at the same time, for
the idea of a perfect commonwealth underlies all rule, and the
idea of paradisial innocence and the golden age provides a point
of reference by which civilization demands to be measured.[1]

Sebastian and Antonio mock Gonzalo, and have no conception of innocence, but can think of his 'subjects' only as idle
'whores and knaves' (l. 160), and when Ariel enters playing the
solemn music which, though not heard by them, puts Alonso,
Gonzalo and the rest to sleep, at once Antonio's 'strong
imagination' (l. 199) works to propose another image of rule.
It is just that as Antonio has driven out Prospero and made
himself Duke of Milan, so may Sebastian get rid of his brother
Alonso and seize the kingdom of Naples. Sebastian sees himself as King for a moment before Ariel comes to wake Gonzalo
and prevent murder:

as thou got'st Milan,
I'll come by Naples. Draw thy sword: one stroke
Shall free thee from the tribute which thou payest;
And I the King shall love thee.

(II.i.282)

Rule for them lies in the mere possession of power, not in the
quality of the man who rules, and in their barbarity they are
worse than Stephano and Caliban, whose plot against Prospero
is conceived in drink rather than in cold blood. The next scene

---

[1] This is elaborated in Leo Marx's brilliant account of the play as 'Shakespeare's
American Fable', in *The Machine in the Garden* (1964), pp. 34-72.

When plot against Pros - drunk/
flattered by civilized people
who should know better unlike
Seb .

shows us these characters. Caliban enters with a load of wood and cursing his master and tormentor who sets his spirits on him to plague him 'for every trifle' (1. 8). He has seen no other human beings besides Prospero and Miranda, and it is natural for him to take Trinculo and Stephano for spirits, just as it is natural for them to regard Caliban as 'some monster of the isle' (l. 62). When Trinculo creeps under Caliban's gaberdine to hide from the storm, they make together a four-legged monster with two mouths which becomes very funny as Stephano converses with both voices at once. The re-appearance of Trinculo, pulled forth by Stephano, serves to emphasize how much less of a 'monster' Caliban himself is. Caliban is described in the list of actors given in the Folio text as 'a salvage and deformed slave', and he has links with Indian savages and cannibals, and with the wild man of European folklore, embodied in drama in such a figure as Bremo of *Mucedorus*; he has been well described in terms developing these basic dimensions:[1]

> His origins and character are natural in the sense that they
> do not partake of grace, civility and art; he is ugly in
> body, associated with an evil natural magic, and unqualified
> for rule or nurture. He exists at the simplest level of sensual
> pain and pleasure, fit for lechery because love is beyond his
> nature, and a natural slave of demons. He hears music with
> pleasure, as music can appeal to the beast who lacks reason;
> and indeed he resembles Aristotle's bestial man.

However, there is more to Caliban as we see him in the action of the play. He not only hears music, but makes it, and his natural medium, it seems, is verse of some distinction, as against the prose of Trinculo and Stephano; also, like the others, he has a sense of the role he might play in the body politic. Prospero is a 'tyrant' (l. 152) to him, and he is glad to change his master, when the new spirits or men he now meets offer him liquor that is not earthly, and through that a vision of freedom. Stephano and Trinculo assume the King is dead, and determine to be rulers of the island, 'we will inherit here' (l. 163), even as Caliban swears allegiance, 'I'll kiss thy foot; I'll swear myself thy subject' (l. 142).

---

[1] Frank Kermode, in his Introduction to *The Tempest*, p. xlii.

In this posture of humility before the drunken butler Stephano, Caliban appears ridiculous to Trinculo, who cries, 'I shall laugh myself to death at this puppy-headed monster' (l. 144); but however absurd and comic he may be here, Caliban retains a kind of superiority over his companions. He knows the qualities of the isle, and without him they would be lost; he has a poetic response to it, and where Trinculo sees a 'most ridiculous monster' (l. 155), we see Caliban vividly and imaginatively reacting to his natural environment as Trinculo never could, and promising to

> Show thee a jay's nest, and instruct thee how
> To snare the nimble marmoset; I'll bring thee
> To clustering filberts, and sometimes I'll get thee
> Young scamels from the rock.

(II.ii.159)

The adjectives 'nimble' and 'clustering' reveal his appreciation of what he has seen. There is something visionary too about Caliban's feeling for freedom, even if he is mistaken in supposing that it will lie in serving Stephano. To him Prospero is the tyrant who robbed him of the island, made use of him, sought to impose his own values and morality on him, and when he rebelled, made him a prisoner and a slave, and any escape from this would be freedom. Prospero taught him language, but Caliban's use of it is his own, and the surprising thing about this is the extent to which Caliban's language matches that of Prospero; Caliban's curses against Prospero are as rich and inventive as Prospero's invective and threats against him in I.ii, and his poetry is every bit as good as that of his master. While, then, we may think of Caliban as in some sense inhuman, and find evidence to support a view of him as almost a beast, as representing the irreducible element of bestiality in human nature,[1] the son of a witch, and, in Prospero's words:

> Thou poisonous slave, got by the devil himself
> Upon thy wicked dam,

(I.ii.319)

[1] See the complex and subtle discussion of Caliban by Kermode, pp. xxiv-xxv and pp. xxxviii-xliii; he sees the extent to which Caliban serves as an 'inverted pastoral hero, against whom civility and the Art which improves Nature may be measured', but still regards him too much in terms of ideas, and not enough in terms of the actor playing the part.

it is not merely this Caliban we are involved with in the action. On the stage we see in the one figure both a brute and a human being (played by an actor like other actors, however disguised), who speaks fine and sophisticated verse, itself a product of both nurture, in his command of language, and nature, in the sensibility he reveals. At first when Prospero made much of him, Caliban 'lov'd' the newcomer to the island, and served Prospero by educating him in 'all the qualities o'th'isle' (I.ii.337); so now in offering to do the same for Stephano, Caliban, kissing the foot of the new master, is expressing, in his kind, his 'love', and this new service seems at first to be perfect freedom.

So the presentation of Caliban here has links with the treatment of Ferdinand in the next scene, who gains a freedom in yielding to the bondage of love, and kneels or makes obeisance of some kind in sign of his service to Miranda ('And I thus humble ever', III.i.87). The analogy continues, however, into the next scene (III.ii), where we find Stephano's 'kingdom' in a state of discord, as he quarrels with Trinculo over Caliban:

> Trinculo, keep a good tongue in your head: if you prove a
> mutineer, – the next tree! The poor monster's my subject, and
> he shall not suffer indignity.
>
> (III.ii.34)

Here, too, we learn that 'freedom' means to Caliban 'revenge' (l. 51) on Prospero for getting the isle by 'sorcery' from him, as he kneels again to Stephano to present his suit, and begs him to kill the 'tyrant'. Caliban's service to his new master is to offer him the opportunity of braining Prospero, and also to 'give' him that nonpareil of beauty Miranda, whom Caliban had wished to possess for himself; and the vision is irresistible for Stephano, 'I will kill this man: his daughter and I will be king and queen – save our graces! – and Trinculo and thyself shall be viceroys' (l. 102). The mood of this scene is different from that of II.ii, as the brutishness of the plot to kill Prospero emerges, and especially in Caliban's images of the deed;

> with a log
> Batter his skull, or paunch him with a stake,
> Or cut his wezand with thy knife.
>
> (III.ii.84)

Yet Caliban retains a kind of superiority over his companions, even in the fuddle of drink which besets them; he makes the scene comic, and takes a good deal of the sting out of their scheming; for his aim is freedom, theirs merely to seize power and rule, and he speaks verse which expresses his sense of beauty and of harmony, while their apprehension is bound by prose.

By this point in the play the drift of the action is settled. Prospero himself has happily witnessed the interchange of vows of love between Ferdinand and Miranda. His spirit Ariel has intervened at Prospero's behest as Sebastian and Antonio were about to murder Alonso and Gonzalo, so that we know these are under supervision. Now Ariel intervenes again, but apparently of his own accord, to promote the quarrel between Stephano and Trinculo, and to lead them astray as they follow his music offstage; here he may, in his capacity as fairy, be 'thwarting the unchaste', as fairies were supposed to 'abhor unchastity',[1] and again he is thwarting a plot of murder. Before the final unravelling and reconciliations of Act V, there now follow two scenes (III.iii and IV.i) in which the focus is on elements corresponding to anti-masque and masque. The play has already provided a sense of spectacle, notably in the opening shipwreck scene, in the way Prospero charms Ferdinand, and as Ariel, 'invisible' to other characters, may control or guide their actions. The island, too, is full of music, the sweet and strange airs of Ariel, whose songs and 'solemn music' suggest order in their power to put men to sleep or wake them, to charm or compel them to follow where the music leads; there are also the drunken songs of Stephano and Caliban, whose 'howling' (II.ii.167) sets up by contrast a discord, and yet, as it is music, both mitigates our sense of their brutishness, and represents the contribution they can make to that quality of the island best appreciated by Caliban:

> the isle is full of noises,
> Sounds and sweet airs, that give delight, and hurt not.
> Sometimes a thousand twangling instruments
> Will hum about mine ears; and sometimes voices,

---

[1] Kermode, *op. cit.*, p. 144. The account he gives of Elizabethan ideas of fairies is based, as he acknowledges, on M. W. Latham's *The Elizabethan Fairies* (1930).

L

That, if I then had wak'd after long sleep,
Will make me sleep again: and then, in dreaming,
The clouds methought would open, and show riches
Ready to drop upon me; that, when I wak'd,
I cried to dream again.

(III.ii.130)

These harmonious sounds of music and voices seem to bring him pleasant dreams and visions, to raise him out of his ordinary existence, even if the scope of his visions is limited to the display of riches about to drop on him.

All this prepares for what in this play is equivalent to a crisis in the action, namely the masque of III.iii to IV.i. In the first of these scenes, Alonso and his companions, with Sebastian and Antonio, weary and frustrated in their search for Ferdinand, and still supposing him drowned, pause to rest; and Antonio and Sebastian think they have a chance to carry out their plot to murder the King and Gonzalo. At this point they see a vision and we see a masque, as, with Prospero placed 'on the top' as a regal spectator, and ultimate creator of what follows, various 'strange shapes' bring in a banquet to 'solemn and strange music'. Gonzalo thinks of these as 'people of the island', and in their 'monstrous shape' (l. 31) they perhaps look like cousins of Caliban, but gentle servants, made in the image of what Prospero would have liked Caliban to be. As Alonso plucks up his courage and makes as if to eat, Ariel, as presenter of the masque, enters 'like a Harpy' in thunder and lightning to clap his monstrous bird's wings upon the table and make it vanish. A harpy as a wind-spirit, and as servant of the Erinyes or avenging Furies is a very appropriate figure for Ariel to take at this point; in his speech addressed to Alonso, Sebastian and Antonio, the 'three men of sin' (l. 53), he speaks to them from within the masque, claiming that he and his fellows are 'ministers of Fate' (l. 61), servants of Destiny, agents of 'The powers' (l. 73). At the same time he speaks to us both as harpy and as Ariel, Prospero's agent, skilfully carrying out his master's instructions, and receiving his congratulations as the business is completed. As the 'shapes' first entered in a dance, so now they return in a dance to carry out the table, and Ariel 'vanishes in thunder'. The men of sin, afflicted with a sense of guilt by the strange vision that demanded of them

> nothing but heart-sorrow
And a clear life ensuing,

(III.iii.81)

show their affliction in 'desperate' behaviour (l. 104); they had drawn their swords when Ariel appeared as a harpy, but were charmed from using them; now, after the vision ends, they run into strange antics, and rush offstage, Alonso in thoughts of drowning, and Sebastian and Antonio fighting imaginary fiends. So the scene ends in disorder and grotesque actions. The whole may be seen as a kind of elaborate anti-masque, in which the monstrous shapes that vanish with grimaces and mocking actions, the harpy, and the disordered rushing about of the men of sin at the end, constitute a driving out of evil, which is to be followed in IV.i by the masque proper.

The punishment Prospero inflicted on Ferdinand turns out to have been but a trial of his love, a kind of symbolic task; by completing it successfully he proves himself fit to marry Miranda, and 'earns' her. As Prospero showed earlier that he had never relinquished his place as ruler of his state by treating Ferdinand as a 'traitor', so now he gives him his daughter within the framework of full social and religious ceremonies:

> If thou dost break her virgin-knot before
> All sanctimonious ceremonies may
> With full and holy rite be minister'd,
> No sweet aspersion shall the heavens let fall . . .

(IV.i.15)

The emphasis on virginity here is often noted, and it is of course important as relating to the moral discipline of the individual, and to the opposition between Miranda's chastity and Caliban's unrestrained lechery; but what is equally important is Prospero's insistence on 'sanctimonious ceremonies', for where is the priest to perform these rites? The normal social, political and religious order of society is assumed in the way Prospero talks. In this context, he bestows on the lovers a vanity of his art in the form of a masque, which, in terms of what a court-masque signifies, has the effect of giving the betrothal a full social sanction, and announcing it publicly.

In fact the masque does more than this. I do not know of any extant masque of this period that is a betrothal masque, though several wedding masques survive, like those for the marriage of Princess Elizabeth in 1613, or Ben Jonson's masque for Lord Harrington's marriage in 1608, or the masque in Beaumont and Fletcher's *The Maid's Tragedy* for the marriage of Amintor and Evadne. The masque in these instances provided a public ceremonious congratulation on the occasion of the union, and although it could, in *The Maid's Tragedy*, be skilfully distorted to foreshadow the darkness and disaster that were to follow in the action of that play, it could also, and especially in the lofty vein of Ben Jonson's conceptions, go far beyond compliment and decorative splendour. In his most sophisticated masques, the expulsion of evil or darkness is followed by a blaze of virtue and light suggesting something beyond happiness or pleasure, and becoming an emblem of order and harmony passing into a hint of universal order and harmony. The dances which formed a central feature of the masque could be very important in this, as is shown by the commentary of the presenter Daedalus, the legendary artist and inventor of the labyrinth of Minos, in *Pleasure Reconciled to Virtue* (1618):

> Then as all actions of mankind
> Are but a labyrinth or maze,
> So let your dances be entwined,
> Yet not perplex men unto gaze;
> But measured, and so numerous too,
> As men may read each act you do,
> And when they see the graces meet,
> Admire the wisdom of your feet;
> For dancing is an exercise
> Not only shows the mover's wit,
> But maketh the beholder wise,
> As he hath power to rise to it.

The dance exhibits through the 'wisdom' of the dancers' feet a pattern in what appears to be a maze, and the beholder who can understand this may be made wise, as he sees an image of order in the intricacies of movement, suggesting that all human actions, though inexplicable and bewildering to us, make a pattern in a larger scheme of order, the cosmic dance, the order of providence. In making Daedalus interpret the dance here in this way, Jonson was exploiting in a sophisticated and complex way a familiar Renaissance analogy, as exemplified in *Orchestra* (?1596), addressed by Sir John Davies to Queen Elizabeth:

> Dancing, bright lady, then began to be,
>   When the first seeds whereof the world did spring,
> The fire, air, earth, and water did agree
>   By love's persuasion, nature's mighty king,
> To leave their first discorded combating,
>   And in a dance such measure to observe,
>   As all the world their motion should preserve.
>
> Since when they still are carried in a round,
>   And changing come one in another's place;
> Yet do they neither mingle nor confound,
>   But every one doth keep the bounded space
> Wherein the dance doth bid it turn or trace.
>   This wondrous miracle did Love devise,
>   For dancing is love's proper exercise.

Dancing as the exercise of love signifies the divine harmony controlling the spheres, the planets in their movements, and all nature. Dancing as 'measure' or order, signifying matrimony, as at the end of so many of Shakespeare's comedies, carries in it hints of a greater harmony or order, that of the heavens.

What Prospero introduces as 'Some vanity of mine Art' (l. 41) would have meant much more than this to audiences at the Globe or Blackfriars. After the grotesque shows and dances of III.iii, ending in the confused rushing about of Alonso, Sebastian and Antonio, there follows now the harmonious masque proper, with Ariel again as presenter, playing, as I take it, the part of Iris. This seems the best interpretation of his phrase at l. 167, 'when I presented Ceres'; and even without this comment, a link between the Harpy of III.iii and Iris might have been suspected. For, according to Hesiod, Iris was the sister of the Harpies, and as Ariel appeared in III.iii with a woman's face and a bird's wings and talons, or, as Shakespeare phrased a simile in *Pericles:*[1]

>   like the harpy,
> Which, to betray, dost with thine angel's face
> Seize with thine eagle's talons,

                                                    (IV.iii.46)

----

[1] The parallel with *Pericles* is cited in Kermode, *op. cit.*, p. 89n.

so now in Iris the same angelic face is seen, but Ariel is dressed to suggest the goddess of the rainbow. Iris, messenger of the gods, and, as rainbow, a link between heaven and earth, summons Ceres, presented here as goddess of harvest and of earth, to attend on Juno, queen of heaven, and like Ceres, a mother-goddess. Their business is first to make sure that Venus and Cupid are at a safe distance, so that no wantonness or lust may attend on the proceedings, and then to 'celebrate A contract of true love' (l. 133). The two goddesses, who are shown as sisters (l. 103), join in song to bless Ferdinand and Miranda, and their song is, in effect, a marriage song:

> *Juno*   Honour, riches, marriage-blessing,
> Long continuance, and increasing,
> Hourly joys be still upon you!
> Juno sings her blessings on you.
> *Ceres*   Earth's increase, foison plenty,
> Barns and garners never empty;
> Vines with clust'ring bunches growing;
> Plants with goodly burthen bowing. . . .
> Ceres' blessing so is on you.
>
> (IV.i.106)

This blessing seems to be the 'donation' (l. 85) they bestow on the lovers, a promise of honour, riches, and fruitfulness. So although the young couple have vowed

> that no bed-right shall be paid
> Till Hymen's torch be lighted,
>
> (IV.i.96)

the masque becomes implicitly a marriage-masque, and as such is indeed, as Ferdinand calls it, a 'most majestic vision' (l. 118).

Juno and Ceres then call on Iris to summon a group of 'temperate nymphs' (l. 132) to join with a group of reapers or 'sunburn'd sicklemen' (l. 134) in a graceful dance linking the Naiads of the water, cool and fresh, with the hot harvesters, weary with August; the union of these perhaps symbolizes the state of marriage, and certainly as a harvest dance their performance is more appropriate to a wedding than a betrothal. At this point Prospero interrupts the masque, and the spirits vanish in a 'strange, hollow, and confused noise'; the stage direction calls for him to intervene 'towards the end' of the dance, and 'interrupts' is perhaps the wrong word to describe his action, for the masque is in fact complete. The 'anti-masque' of the monstrous shapes and men of sin in III.iii gives way to a harmonious vision looking forward to prosperity, honour and a blessed life for Ferdinand and Miranda; it offers them congratulation, compliment, and closes with a dance of reapers and nymphs, symbolizing the union of ripeness with temperance in marriage. It is so compelling as a vision that Prospero loses himself in it, and forgets the 'foul conspiracy' of Caliban and his companions, so that the 'confused noise' and discords heard at the end of the masque represent the troubled mind of Prospero, and do not reflect on the masque except to show again that it is in one sense a projection of Prospero's mind or 'art'. On another level we share the lovers' acceptance of it as a splendid vision, harmonious and wise; and we see it also as a real masque enacted by performers on a stage.

It is true that one element of the conventional masque, that final stage in which the masquers 'take out' spectators into the dance and make them participants, is lacking here. Ferdinand and Miranda are kept at a distance from it as onlookers, so that they will see it as a vision acted out by spirits raised by Prospero's art. This is how Prospero himself speaks of it too, notably in his famous speech to Ferdinand:

Our revels now are ended. These our actors,
As I foretold you, were all spirits, and
Are melted into air, into thin air:
And, like the baseless fabric of this vision,
The cloud-capp'd towers, the gorgeous palaces,
The solemn temples, the great globe itself,
Yea, all which it inherit, shall dissolve,
And, like this insubstantial pageant faded,
Leave not a rack behind. We are such stuff
As dreams are made on; and our little life
Is rounded with a sleep.

(IV.i.148)

There has been much discussion of this speech as a comment in particular on masques, and in general on human life and the mutability of all things; but if in one perspective life itself appears no more than an 'insubstantial pageant' like the masque, a fleeting vision or dream, in another perspective the pageant is most substantial, and reflects a view of life as rich and significant. For this vision or masque is itself an imaginative achievement of a high order, combining visual spectacle, poetry, music and dance in an art-form which emerges out of centuries of civilization and concern for the flowering of the human spirit. Moreover, the descent of Juno as queen of heaven constitutes a theophany in the play corresponding in some measure with the theophanies in *Cymbeline* (the descent of Jupiter), and in *The Winter's Tale* (the coming to life of the statue-goddess in the figure of Hermione). In this sense, the masque relates to an order outside Prospero, and beyond his control, a heavenly order. The masque belongs in a scheme of social and cosmic order to which Prospero himself subscribes, as is shown by his determination that the wedding of the lovers shall be celebrated with 'full and holy rite', in his ratifying his gift of Miranda to Ferdinand 'afore Heaven' (l. 7), and in his concern throughout to restore himself to his rightful place as Duke of Milan. As vision and performance the masque passes and melts into air, but as theophany and as a masque full of substance seen by the audience, it contradicts the notion of human insignificance in Prospero's phrase, 'our little life Is rounded with a sleep'.

In his admiration of the vision Prospero has his spirits enact, and of his prospective father-in-law as magician, artist, poet, choreographer and producer, Ferdinand cries:

> Let me live here ever;
> So rare a wonder'd father and a wise
> Makes this place Paradise.
>
> (IV.i.122)

The vision renews the image of Ferdinand and Miranda as first man and first woman, or Adam and Eve figures, recalling her first thought of him as a 'thing divine', and his sense of her as 'goddess' (I.ii.418, 421). Human beings cannot remain for ever in paradise, or in what the masque of Juno and Ceres hints at, the golden world of pastoral; these belong to visions, dreams, poetical 'fancies', to use Prospero's word (l. 122). Ferdinand has already had to endure a temporary loss of 'paradise' in the hard labour of log-bearing, and must return again to the workaday world. So Caliban's vision of Stephano as a 'brave god' (II.ii.109), and Gonzalo's fancy of an ideal commonwealth, dissolve and leave not a rack behind. Yet the visions and dreams are real, if transitory, and work, as by analogy the whole play, Shakespeare's 'vision', does, to open vistas on higher possibilities and orderings of human life. At the same time, they link with the masque-like elements in the play and come to a focus in the great masque of IV.i to insist on the artifice of the incredible fiction which composes the play's action. But paradoxically, this masque, as theophany, in the substance of what it says, and by its social function, both affirms an order in the heavens beyond Prospero's art, and firmly returns us to the social order, as it looks to a future of riches and honour for the young couple, and to the formal celebration of the marriage-rites it, so to speak, assumes in advance. It thus reinforces what is the primary drive in the play, the return of Prospero to his proper place in Milan, as he has been waiting for the day when it would be possible for this most civilized of Shakespeare's characters to recover his role in the civilization to which he belongs.[1]

The confused noise at the end of the masque marks Prospero's recollection of his role as 'king' of the island, and the need to take action against the 'foul conspiracy' of Caliban and his companions; the harmony of the vision or masque gives way to a display of passion by Prospero, whom Miranda has never seen so 'touch'd with anger' (l. 145). The large perspective from which 'our little life' appears no more than a dream is replaced by the immediate view of practical life, with its urgencies, passions, and its important moral and social meanings. Prospero becomes again 'compos'd of harshness', as Ferdinand saw him in III.i, when he puts down the rebellion of Stephano. Caliban discovers what fools his companions are, to be diverted from their plot by the 'trumpery' hung up on show by Ariel; a wardrobe fit for a king becomes more important to them than the kingdom itself, and Caliban's remonstrance is turned aside by Stephano with the threat, 'help to bear this away . . . or I'll

---

[1] Many commentaries on *The Tempest* ignore the masque of Ceres, or regard it as of little consequence. I have come across two accounts of the play which see it as of central importance structurally; one is by R. J. Nelson, *Play Within a Play* (1958), pp. 30-5, who sees the mood of *The Tempest* as shifting 'from the comic to the tragic or something akin to it' after the masque; the other is the fine analysis of the masque and its links with pastoral by Leo Marx in *The Machine in the Garden*, pp. 61-5, to which I am indebted.

turn you out of my kingdom' (l. 249). At this point Prospero and Ariel enter like hunters to set a pack of 'Spirits, in shape of dogs and hounds' upon them, two of them bearing the names 'Fury' and 'Tyrant'. The hounds embody the wrath of Prospero, and something like vindictiveness, as he congratulates himself on having all his 'enemies' at his mercy, and summons goblins to torture Stephano, Trinculo and Caliban, and 'grind their joints With dry convulsions' (l. 257).

Now, at the beginning of Act V, Ariel reports on the King, Alonso, and his followers, and by a nice touch prompts Prospero to mercy:

> Your charm so strongly works 'em
> That if you now beheld them, your affections
> Would become tender.
>
> (V.i.17)

Prospero accepts the hint, and, while admitting to 'fury', the word echoing the name of the hound in the previous scene, he renounces his anger:

> Though with their high wrongs I am struck to th'quick,
> Yet with my nobler reason 'gainst my fury
> Do I take part: the rarer action is
> In virtue than in vengeance.
>
> (V.i.25)

Here 'pardon' would be the obvious word, rather than 'virtue',[1] which, however, is much stronger, as implying his desire to make his conduct conform to moral laws, and indirectly invoking a Christian sanction for his action. The climax has arrived, the moment when Prospero can renounce too his magic, and reclaim his place in society. He has another great speech here, matching in poignancy and resonance his dismissal of the masque, with the lines beginning 'Our revels now are ended'; both speeches express a kind of farewell, and both are moving, with their mood of regret and resignation, nostalgia for pleasures that have passed, and acceptance of what must be. They are, however, very different in kind; the first speech marks the end of a majestic vision which embodies the highest imaginative working of Prospero's magic art, even if it is in one aspect a

---

[1] A point noted by Kermode, p. 114.

mere show or 'vanity'; the second speech follows on from the display of another sort of magic, in which Prospero hunts his enemies with spirits in the shape of hounds. It is based on the incantation of the witch Medea in Ovid's *Metamorphoses*, and although it has been argued that 'only those elements which are consistent with "white" magic are taken over for Prospero',[1] this is to make a dubious, and from the point of view of an audience watching the play, oversubtle distinction. For the speech shows Prospero excited by, and almost boasting about, feats of 'rough magic' such as we have not seen him perform:

> I have bedimm'd
> The noontide sun, call'd forth the mutinous winds,
> And 'twixt the green sea and the azur'd vault
> Set roaring war: to the dread rattling thunder
> Have I given fire, and rifted Jove's stout oak
> With his own bolt; the strong-bas'd promontory
> Have I made shake, and by the spurs pluck'd up
> The pine and cedar: graves at my command
> Have wak'd their sleepers, op'd, and let 'em forth
> By my so potent Art. But this rough magic
> I here abjure. . . .
>
> (V.i.41)

We have seen him create a storm and shipwreck, but only for the special purpose of distributing the boat's crew and passengers about the isle, and we have seen Prospero use his powers to confine, hunt, and torment his 'slaves' and 'enemies'; but here, for the first time, we learn of his delight in using his magic for its own sake, to disturb the natural order, and make discord and destruction in ways traditionally associated with witchcraft. So, for example, his power over the 'mutinous winds', to make them serve him, was commonly attributed to witches, and is made much of in *Macbeth*, where the First Witch proposes to punish a sailor by using winds to toss his boat with tempests, and where Macbeth later tries to compel the Witches to answer him, crying:

> Though you untie the winds, and let them fight
> Against the churches; though the yesty waves
> Confound and swallow navigation up. . . .
>
> (IV.i.52)

[1] Kermode, *op. cit.*, p. 149.

His words sufficiently anticipate Prospero's lines to indicate how far the latter moves towards traditional claims for witchcraft in a speech which ends with the most sinister statement of all, that he has brought back the dead from the grave, a feat for which Dr Faustus was well known.

At this point in the play Shakespeare seems to emphasize Prospero's connection with black magic deliberately, as indeed there can have been no graves on the isle for him to open. Prospero has the mantle and staff proper to the magician; he has forced Ariel, in return for a promise of his freedom, to bind himself as his servant for a specific length of time (I.ii.245); and we have seen him in anger use his magic to cruel effect. At the same time, we have the overriding sense of Prospero as a practiser of white magic, and of his major effort to restore order and harmony. This seeming contradiction is resolved in the distinction between magic and the magician; in other words, *The Tempest* does not offer a sharp clash between black magic and white magic, but offers rather a sense of magic as an art at best neutral, and perhaps dubious in its common use, but available to good or bad ends, depending on the user. Prospero is sometimes seen as a neo-Platonic mage, 'whose Art is to achieve supremacy over the natural world by holy magic', and who renounces his 'rough magic' as a stage in his enlightenment and ascension to the 'First Cause', in the phrase of Cornelius Agrippa.[1] In fact, Agrippa, whose book on *Occult Philosophy* provides an apologia for white magic, was popularly known as a black magician, and probably gave his name to Cornelius, one of the advisers of Doctor Faustus in Marlowe's play, in which the hero looks forward to becoming:

> as cunning as Agrippa was,
> Whose shadows made all Europe honour him.

(I.i.116)

The allusion is to Agrippa's supposed ability to summon up the dead, a power which Prospero also claims to possess. All magic tends to look like black magic, and *The Tempest* shows Prospero's passionate and difficult endeavour to control his art by controlling himself. The art itself is the same in kind as that practised by the witch Sycorax, a point made effectively

---

[1] See Kermode, *op. cit.*, pp. xl-xli.

early in the play, when Prospero, having told us how he released Ariel from the twelve years' imprisonment in a cloven pine inflicted on him by Sycorax, goes on almost immediately to threaten his 'brave spirit' with a corresponding punishment:

> If thou more murmur'st, I will rend an oak,
> And peg thee in his knotty entrails, till
> Thou hast howl'd away twelve winters.

(I.ii.294)

The difference lies in the way the art is used, and Prospero's is higher and more potent than that of Sycorax because the orders he gives to his ministers are proper for a spirit

too delicate

> To act her earthy and abhorr'd commands.

(I.ii.272)

The harmonious vision of the masque, the finest product of Prospero's magic art, ends in a blaze of intense emotion for him, as he recalls Caliban, and is reminded that the ideal, the dream, is no more than a dream, denied by the very existence of brute forces exemplified in this 'born devil' and his murderous plot. Prospero's farewell now to his 'rough magic' ends, by contrast, with the sound of 'heavenly music', as Ariel brings Alonso and his companions into a magic circle. As one ends with a reminder of the need to control Caliban, so the other ends with the return of Ariel, and Prospero recalling his obligation to set free his 'dainty' spirit. Even as Ariel helps Prospero to put on his ducal clothes, and show himself as he 'was sometime Milan' (V.i.85), in the full acceptance of his social role and its obligations, Ariel sings his song of freedom, 'Where the bee sucks, there suck I', and Prospero cries:

> Why, that's my dainty Ariel! I shall miss thee;
> But yet thou shalt have freedom.

(V.i.95)

Here Ariel seems to be associated with those fancies Prospero could give rein to on the island, as in the vision of the masque, but which, as ruler of Milan, he must henceforth curb; so Ariel is liberated to live merrily in a world of flowers. Ariel is, of course, more than this, as he is a 'familiar', bound by a pact to serve Prospero in a relationship that has in it elements of black magic. Ariel in this aspect is essentially independent of Prospero and of human beings, as a spirit or fairy, a 'tricksy spirit', at times mischievous, and able to work for good or evil. In bidding farewell to his 'rough magic', Prospero is renouncing a power which has given him pleasure, and which could serve black ends. It is appropriate that this speech, with its mood of regret combined with a sense of willing abjuration, should lead directly into the final resolution of the action, and the recovery for Prospero of his full role in society.

Ariel carries out his last tasks, to bring Alonso and the courtiers into the presence of Prospero, then the crew of the ship, and finally Caliban, Stephano and Trinculo. As Alonso and his companions 'stand charm'd' in a magic circle, Prospero changes his costume, removing his magician's robe:

> I will discase me, and myself present
> As I was sometime Milan

(V.i.85)

At this point Prospero assumes royal authority again, as the group on stage suggests a tableau of his court, an image he realizes in dialogue a little later, as the courtiers emerge from their initial 'wonder and amazement', and he welcomes Alonso:

> Welcome, sir;
> This cell's my court: here have I few attendants,
> And subjects none abroad.

(V.i.165)

Wonder is to be renewed and strengthened, as more is revealed; first, Alonso experiences another 'vision of the island' (l. 176), his first thought being that he is seeing another illusion, like the 'shapes' of III.iii, when Prospero 'discovers' Ferdinand and Miranda playing chess. It is the more wonderful that this really is his son Alonso sees, and a girl he cannot but think for a moment is a 'goddess' (l. 187), just as Miranda, seeing the group of courtiers for the first time, exclaims 'O wonder!' There is more to come, as the Boatswain and crew enter 'amazedly following' Ariel, and Alonso cries:

> These are not natural events; they strengthen
> From strange to stranger.

(V.i.227)

Finally, Caliban, Stephano and Trinculo are driven in, to modify the image of a brave new world seen by Miranda, and perhaps by Alonso, as both Stephano and Trinculo are reeling in drink, and more bestial than Caliban, who realizes now what a fool he has been 'to take this drunkard for a god, And worship this dull fool!' (l. 296).

It is tempting to take Gonzalo's words as a general comment on this scene, and indeed, as some would have it, on the play:

> O, rejoice
> Beyond a common joy! and set it down
> With gold on lasting pillars: in one voyage
> Did Claribel her husband find at Tunis,
> And Ferdinand, her brother, found a wife,
> Where he himself was lost, Prospero his dukedom
> In a poor isle, and all of us ourselves
> Where no man was his own.
>
> (V.i.206)

Earlier, in II.i, his sense of the island as 'lush and lusty' (II.i.49) had led him to develop his vision of the ideal commonwealth, a new golden age, on it, even as Sebastian and Antonio mocked him, seeing the island as uninhabitable desert and rotten fen; and now, as then, Gonzalo's sentiments are noble, but his vision a partial one. Not only does Antonio remain silent throughout this scene, as if aloof and unchanged, not sharing in repentance or wonder, but also there is little sign that Sebastian has found himself, while the last episode brings on Stephano and Trinculo lost in drink, and Caliban. Alonso must 'know and own' his drunken servants, even as Prospero accepts responsibility for Caliban:

> Two of these fellows you
> Must know and own; this thing of darkness I
> Acknowledge mine.
>
> (V.i.274)

Caliban becomes, momentarily, part of Prospero, an emblem of the evil subdued in himself, but also, in a larger sense, is seen, with his drunken companions, to be part of the body politic, and presumably is to return with Prospero to Milan; and however Caliban may hope to 'be wise hereafter, And seek for grace' (l. 294), there seems to be no expectation of a change in him by

Prospero, whose last words about him are to call him 'demi-devil' and 'thing of darkness'.

Gonzalo describes well enough what one might call the nominal resolution of the action in accordance with the experience of many of the characters, as they have moved from shipwreck, loss and disharmony, to recovery, joy, and harmony. The drive of Prospero to recover rule in himself and in his dukedom has shaped the play, and is now fulfilled. On a deeper level the ending is less simple and comfortable than Gonzalo's image of it, and underneath the joy and restoration of the last scene, the force of the paradoxes established by the play remains held in suspension. Only by exile from Milan, from civilization, does Prospero learn how to rule, by being somehow refreshed and restored by the new world of a primitive island, on which he may be seen as regaining 'access to sources of vitality and truth'.[1] There, in what may be seen as a desert wilderness or a kind of Arcadia, if one accepts the view of either Sebastian or Gonzalo in II.i, and which in fact contains both, Prospero tames nature by his art, establishes what civilization he can, and learns the uses of power. His contact with Arcadia and the possibility of an ideal commonwealth as envisaged by Gonzalo, his return to nature, only serves to teach him the necessity of rule. The innocent native of the desert Arcadia proves to be the brutish Caliban, in whom man's sensual impulses have free range; and if a return to Arcadia can restore the image of the golden age to the good, but somewhat naïve, old Gonzalo, and growing up there can give Miranda a fresh and golden image of the first men she sees:

> How beauteous mankind is! O brave new world,
> That has such people in't!

(V.i.183)

At the same time it serves to remind Prospero of the beast in man too, that the thing of darkness is his, and only through the struggles to achieve inward rule has he succeeded in establishing outward order. As Caliban discovers that service to Prospero ('I'll be wise hereafter, And seek for grace') is more like freedom than liberty as the subject of Stephano, so Ferdinand and Miranda learn to renounce their freedom in the

---

[1] Leo Marx *op. cit.*, p. 69.

voluntary bondage of love, a paradox emblematized as Prospero discovers them playing chess, a game at which the sexes meet as equals, and which had been often allegorized in terms of the courtship of two lovers making their moves in turn, and also in terms of life itself, as the chessmen 'stand for the different ranks and occupations of men'.[1] The game in which they may, as Miranda puts it, wrangle 'for a score of kingdoms', is serious as it ends in mate; their love-play bears on their relation to come as husband and wife, and as prince and princess, rulers of men.

At the centre of the play the masque of IV.i serves as a focus for these paradoxes. The masque in a sense realizes as a vision Gonzalo's idea of the golden age, in the image of Ceres and Juno together offering a prospect of perpetual natural plenty, and echoing Spenser's Garden of Adonis:

Spring come to you at the farthest
In the very end of harvest!

(IV.i.114)

There is continuall spring, and harvest there
Continuall, both meeting at one time. . . .

(*The Faerie Queene*, III.vi.42)

However, this is not Gonzalo's primitive world of innocence, a sort of Eden where society might begin over again in a new setting of unspoiled nature, but rather the end-product of an age-old civilization, embodied in the highest imaginative reach of Prospero's art.[2] The masque is a court entertainment, of a stylized and highly structured kind, which contains the vision of innocence within a pattern involving tradition, myth, history, and social obligation; the pastoral scene itself is no longer primitive, but cultivated with

rich leas
Of wheat, rye, barley, vetches, oats and pease,

(IV.i.61)

and the whole masque is designed to celebrate a contract of true love in betrothal pointing to marriage. It is the most sophisticated version of pastoral in the late plays, and though

[1] H. J. R. Murray, *A History of Chess* (1913). p. 533; see also pp. 435-7.
[2] Leo Marx, *op. cit.*, p. 62, sees the setting as 'an idealized version of Old England'.

M

only a 'vanity', an 'insubstantial pageant', it is as substantial and 'real' as the 'reality' of the world of Naples and Milan to which the play returns us at the end. It is the vision, like the other wonders and games contrived by art, that gives that social and political world its bearings, enables it to understand the relation between nature and civilization, and illustrates the necessity and nature of rule; and finally, it images the moral and religious sanctions necessary for society.

The marriage of Ferdinand to Miranda, and the return to Milan, will complete all that Prospero aimed to do; the drive that has sustained him is exhausted. His art is no longer necessary, and the emotional power of his farewell to it is bound up with the larger farewell to the island, and, in a sense, to his life. All the years on the island were a preparation for a return to Milan, and for the proper restoration of his daughter to her place in society, and these things achieved, Prospero has made his masterpiece, and the rest is preparation for death; so he says that in Milan:

Every third thought shall be my grave.

(V.i.311)

The epilogue wittily continues this image, as he comes to beg the favour of the audience:

Now I want
Spirits to enforce, Art to enchant;
And my ending is despair,
Unless I be reliev'd by prayer.

His 'ending' is the death of the magician, conventionally dying, like Faustus, in despair, unless his prayers can save him and win the indulgence of the audience. This perhaps confirms that final paradox for Prospero, that the success of his art in completing all his desires is also the completion of his life, in the sense that it leaves him nothing more to live for; which accounts for the sense of melancholy that many people carry away from what is superficially a joyful ending.[1]

---

[1] David Grene in *Reality and the Heroic Pattern* (1967) registers especially sharply his feeling that 'a play which is an uninterrupted story of success for its chief actor leaves one with the prevailing sense of melancholy and failure' (p. 100). I do not share his view, but his essay deserves attention as a sensitive reading of the play.

5

Epilogue:
A note on *King Henry VIII*

In a fundamental sense, *King Henry VIII* is a natural sequel to *The Tempest*. This can be said without nagging again at the vexed question of authorship, for no one has ever doubted that those crucial scenes which establish the shape of the play, in particular the opening scenes, the trial of Katherine (II.iv), the setting-up of the fall of Wolsey in the first half of III.ii, and the trial of Cranmer (V.i) were all written by Shakespeare. The rest follows inevitably from these scenes, and Shakespeare planned the play, even if he did not write every word of it.[1] His plan 'seems to illustrate in plausible historical terms the application of the spirit in which *The Tempest* was written to the actual events of the English sixteenth century'.[2] Both plays may be distinguished in this respect from *Cymbeline* and *The Winter's Tale*. These are primarily designed to display human activities governed by fortune and chance under the operation of an inscrutable providence, and within many of the conventions of

[1] See my Introduction to the New Arden edition of *King Henry VIII* (1957, revised, and with a further note on the authorship, 1964), pp. xvii-xxviii. See also Samuel Schoenbaum, *Internal Evidence and Elizabethan Dramatic Authorship* (1966), pp. 128-30 and Thomas Clayton's long review article on this book in *Shakespeare Studies*, IV (1968), especially pp. 355-74.

[2] Cited from H. M. Richmond's essay, 'Shakespeare's Henry VIII: Romance Redeemed by History', Shakespeare Studies, IV (1968), p. 336. I am indebted to this stimulating essay, which is an important study of the play.

romance, and they are both plays set in pagan times, whatever Christian resonances sound in them.[1] *The Tempest* and *King Henry VIII* are both, by contrast, plays set in effect in modern times, and in the Christian context of the Duchy of Milan, or the Kingdom of England; and both are designed to display human activities within the framework of government or rule.

Most of the characters of *The Tempest* seem occupied by thoughts of ruling a kingdom; Caliban and Stephano would be king of the island, and Sebastian is ambitious to rule in Naples; Gonzalo imagines his utopian kingdom, and Ferdinand thinks of himself as King of Naples. At the centre is Prospero, who has 'usurped' upon the island, and at the same time is rightful king in so far as the matter of ruling is shown by the play's action to turn on 'finding' oneself, knowing oneself, and so being able to rule oneself. The true exercise of power stems from self-rule, the discipline learned with difficulty by Prospero. If any of Shakespeare's characters can be said to represent his ideal king, then Prospero is the one; but he rules an imaginary kingdom with the aid of magic. Ideal kings do not belong to history. In *King Henry VIII* the action focuses on the exigencies of ruling England, that is to say, not on self-rule and the exercise of power so much as on the fumbling inadequacies of men and their laws in a given historical situation. These inadequacies are made good in the end by the generosity of providence in the promise of the infant Elizabeth:

> This royal infant (heaven still move about her)
> Though in her cradle, yet now promises
> Upon this land a thousand thousand blessings
> Which time shall bring to ripeness.

(V.iv.17)

---

[1] Much criticism is devoted to accounting for the last plays in explicitly Christian terms; recent studies of this kind include R. G. Hunter's *Shakespeare and the Comedy of Forgiveness* (1965), and Homer Swander's '*Cymbeline*: Religious Idea and Dramatic Design', in *Pacific Coast Studies in Shakespeare*, edited by Waldo McNeir and Thelma Greenfield (1966), pp. 248-62. There are, of course, many biblical echoes and religious undertones in these plays; it would be surprising if there were not, considering when they were written. But these echoes and undertones belong to that general context of the plays which audiences have always taken for granted, and are not a special part of their dramatic structure. There is no basis 'for arguing for overt theological intent on Shakespeare's part', as has been well shown by Naseeb Shaheen in 'The Use of Scripture in *Cymbeline*', *Shakespeare Studies*, IV (1968), 294-315. The quotation is from p. 310.

Here the emphasis is on the nature of rule, rather than the nature of the ruler, as the play takes for granted the failures and limitations of governors as men. It is also, as a play about recent history, centrally concerned with 'truth', and this marks an important departure from the plays that precede it. It was known by the alternative title, 'All is True', according to the letter of Sir Henry Wotton describing the burning of the Globe at a performance of it in the summer of 1613.[1] The prologue takes up this theme, stressing the intention of the players to offer a serious drama, one which will show 'our chosen truth', and which, indeed, proposes to offer nothing but the truth:

> To make that only true we now intend. . . .
> Be sad, as we would make ye. Think ye see
> The very persons of our noble story
> As they were living.

However, the truth is not simple, or easily arrived at, and the nature of 'truth' is as central an issue in the action as is the business of 'rule'. This is brought out structurally in the play by the constant sense of spectacle, not merely in pageantry, though this is very important, but in the public shows men make of themselves to each other. The action turns on what men observe, how they see one another, how they interpret and misinterpret, and often go wrong. The play has several walking gentlemen, onlookers upon events and actions involving others, and a number of lords like Norfolk, Suffolk and the Lord Chamberlain, as well as the Old Lady and Butts, whose function is primarily to comment on what they see; but these are not merely peripheral characters, for their varying perspectives contribute to the very substance of the action. Views of the same event may differ radically, as we discover in the opening scene. Norfolk, overwhelmed by the splendours of the meeting of Charles and Henry at the Field of the Cloth of Gold, reviews it enthusiastically as an occasion of royal splendour and patriotic achievement, in which the English satisfactorily matched the French; in Buckingham's view, however, the whole business merely reflects the ambition and pride of its organizer,

---

[1] Wotton said, 'The Kings Players had a new play called *All is True*, representing some principal pieces of the Reign of Henry 8'; see the New Arden edition, p. 180.

Wolsey. The 'truth' of an event or action is not clear, but remains to be assessed in the light of differing views and interpretations of it.

This is shown more elaborately in the fall of Buckingham. In I.ii Henry we hear the charges brought against him by his surveyor. Katherine, who is present, doubts the veracity of the witness, who is prompted by Wolsey; but there is a *prima facie* case against Buckingham, who is called

> to present trial; if he may
> Find mercy in the law, 'tis his.

(I.ii.211)

A legal trial, however, is merely another, and the most testing, occasion on which a variety of perspectives of the same event or person are assessed, in the light of 'evidence' which itself is subject to human error. In the circumstances, as this play presents them, men do the best they can to achieve justice. Buckingham apparently has a fair trial, and is sentenced in due process of law:

> The law I bear no malice for my death,
> 'T has done upon the premisses but justice.

(II.i.62)

Yet he knows his fall has been engineered, and the two gentlemen who watch the procession taking him to the scaffold are confident that Wolsey has plotted it, as they offer another perspective on both men:

> All the commons
> Hate him perniciously, and o'my conscience
> Wish him ten fathom deep; this duke as much
> They love and dote on: call him bounteous Buckingham,
> The mirror of all courtesy.

(II.i.49)

'Bounteous' Buckingham may still be a traitor; all the perspectives may in some sense be true, but clearly no one view contains more than a partial truth. It is in this way that the play establishes its tonality and pattern of expectations.

The trial of Katherine grows out of that of Buckingham. Already in II.i the Second Gentleman sees her fall coming:

> Either the cardinal,
> Or some about him near, have, out of malice
> To the good queen, possess'd him with a scruple
> That will undo her.

(II.i.156)

Henry has been too much heated by the beauty of Anne Boleyn, and this is a factor in the business; but yet his 'scruple' about his marriage is genuine too, and is a perspective presented to us in II.ii, where he 'draws the curtain and sits reading pensively' in the view of Suffolk and Norfolk, who note that 'he is much afflicted' by an anguish, it seems, of spirit. They see Wolsey as swollen in pride and impudence, and as imposing a 'slavery' on them (II.ii.41), but to Henry he is 'The quiet of my wounded conscience' (II.ii.74). Again both perspectives are valid in their way. No one blames the king, who is, one might say, infected like Leontes, so that in the sway of Wolsey he is bound to judge wrongly. So 'history is here made to throw up examples resembling even such gross conduct as Leontes' repudiation of his queen.'[1] The difference in *King Henry VIII* is that no oracle can be consulted, that all the forms of law are properly observed, and that Henry never seems blinded to the excellent qualities of Katherine. All the same, the law here palpably fails to do her 'right and justice', and she is wronged in the divorce. Yet the 'truth' of what happens remains unclear; the variety of perspectives does not permit a simple judgment. Masters rely on servants, and as Buckingham is betrayed by his, so Henry is led astray by Wolsey, and is later fortunate to find a faithful servant in Cranmer. This is not to exonerate him of blame, but to emphasize that the evidence is always conflicting, and a variety of prejudices, motives, feelings and interpretations comes into play.

This is brought out most sharply in the last scene in which Katherine appears; looking to death herself, she learns that Wolsey has died, and speaks her mind about him:

> He was a man
> Of an unbounded stomach, ever ranking
> Himself with princes; one that by suggestion
> Tied all the kingdom; simony was fair play;

---

[1] Richmond, *loc. cit.*, p. 343.

His own opinion was his law: i'th' presence
He would say untruths, and be ever double
Both in his words and meaning. He was never
(But where he meant to ruin) pitiful:
His promises were, as he then was, mighty,
But his performance, as he is now, nothing:
Of his own body he was ill, and gave
The clergy ill example.

(IV.ii.33)

Katherine's accusations go beyond what the play has dealt with, and there have been the merest hints of Wolsey's simony and lechery hitherto; nevertheless, her attack seems, in general, to be justified. However, Griffith, the Queen's faithful attendant, at once seeks to leave to present another view:

This cardinal,
Though from an humble stock, undoubtedly
Was fashioned to much honour. From his cradle
He was a scholar, and a ripe and good one,
Exceeding wise, fair-spoken and persuading:
Lofty and sour to them that lov'd him not,
But to those men that sought him, sweet as summer.
And though he were unsatisfied in getting
(Which was a sin) yet in bestowing, madam,
He was most princely: ever witness for him
Those twins of learning that he rais'd in you,
Ipswich and Oxford; one of which fell with him,
Unwilling to outlive the good that did it,
The other (though unfinish'd) yet so famous,
So excellent in art, and still so rising,
That Christendom shall ever speak his virtue.
His overthrow heap'd happiness upon him,
For then, and not till then, he felt himself,
And found the blessedness of being little;
And to add greater honours to his age
Than man could give him, he died fearing God.

(IV.ii.48)

Again, the play has made nothing of the fact that Wolsey had been the founder of colleges at Ipswich and Oxford, but there has been a hint, and indeed much more than a hint, of most of the good qualities mentioned. Both speeches are based on passages in Holinshed's account of Wolsey after his death in

1530, but in the chronicle they are unrelated to one another, and furthermore, they are separated by many pages and by six years in time from the report of the last days of Katherine. It was by the deliberate design of the dramatist, rearranging history, that these two pictures of Wolsey were brought together.[1]

Which of these portraits is the more faithful? The point surely is that both are in some sense 'true'. Katherine, however, goes on to extend the notion of 'truth' that can contain varying and even opposite perspectives, or rather to suggest another meaning for the word; she says to Griffith,

> Whom I most hated living, thou hast made me,
> With thy religious truth and modesty,
> Now in his ashes honour.
>
> (IV.ii.73)

She introduces a further dimension in the notion of 'religious truth'. 'Religious' could merely mean 'scrupulous', but I think it is more than that here, as Katherine accepts Griffith's version as in the end the right one, and so points to a final sense in which all in this play may be 'true'. The religious truth is, on one level, the most charitable interpretation of men and events, seeing what is good in them; but it is also the sense of providence operating through men and events, that sense which enables Katherine to bless Henry and the infant Elizabeth in spite of her own suffering. It manifests itself in the blessed vision granted to her a few moments after she speaks of 'religious truth', and again in Cranmer's prophecy at the end of the play.

So human actions are liable to appear to men in the light of Wolsey's comment early on, when he defends the levy he is making on the King's subjects as not his own particular measure, but the result of a unanimous vote:

> What we oft do best,
> By sick interpreters (once weak ones) is
> Not ours or not allow'd; what worst, as oft

---

[1] Katherine's speech is based on a passage in Holinshed's *Chronicles* (1587), III, 922; Griffith's on a passage from p. 917. The visit of Capuchius to Katherine is reported on p. 939. Wolsey died in 1530, Katherine in 1536. Griffith attends Katherine at her trial in Holinshed, but does not appear at Kimbolton; Shakespeare brought him into this scene, and also invented the character of Patience in it, Katherine's gentlewoman.

Hitting a grosser quality, is cried up
For our best act.

(I.ii.81)

At the same time, interpretation may not only err, but be in any case incomplete, if it falls short of 'religious truth'. The best that men can do in their daily workings is to rely on the help of fortune or heaven's grace to make good their limitations, and open perspectives on a better truth. This may come in self-discovery, as Wolsey learns to know himself, or in discovery of errors, or plots, or misconduct, as when the cardinal's letters to the Pope miscarry, and come 'to th'eye o'the king', so that Henry cannot help understanding his schemes – evidence that is confirmed when Wolsey accidentally sends an inventory of his own wealth to the king. Rule is necessary, but kings, as Henry is an example, have to operate within the limited perspectives of all men, and rely on the observation of others in their judgments and decisions, so that they are bound to be wrong or mistaken sometimes. The instruments of rule, the king's servants, the law itself, may all enact injustices, as they make Katherine suffer, even as, by a happier working of events, Wolsey's treachery is revealed, and Cranmer is saved from his enemies. In the play 'religious truth' prevails, in the glow of the ending, with its promise of peace, plenty and love, and its sense that all errors and sufferings find a compensation in heaven's blessing on the realm; the play ends with festivity, not merely 'holiday', but, as Henry says:

This little one shall make it Holy-day.

One interpretation of the play's design suggests that Henry as the focal figure ultimately emerges into self-awareness and authority 'through a plausible series of historical errors of judgment', and that he grows in stature as the play goes on.[1] The emphasis this puts on Henry, making him the central character, is surely correct, but it would be a mistake to think of this as an effect simply brought about by the arrangement of the play's action, culminating in the fall of Wolsey, the arrival

[1] As I argued in my Introduction to the New Arden edition (1964), pp. lxi-lxii, and as Richmond also claims, p. 347, in a passage from which the quotation here is taken.

of Cranmer, and the birth of the future Queen Elizabeth. Certainly the play illustrates that on one level nothing changes, as rulers, like other men, operate within limited perspectives, and must dwell in uncertainties, registered in the play in Henry's nervous, explosive trick of speech, that questioning 'Ha?' Rule is necessary and good, and all accept Henry gratefully as king, but it is left to Heaven to correct his mistakes. At the same time, it is important to ask whether there is a turning-point in the structure, a point at which Henry begins to emerge into the panoply of kingship. There is such a point, I think, at the end of II.iv, after the trial of Katherine, when Henry watches her leave the court, and praises her warmly. The initiative rests with Wolsey, who, instead of getting on with the business in hand, the proceedings for the divorce, makes a tactical error: his self-centredness drives him to press the king to clear his name:

> I require your highness,
> That it shall please you to declare in hearing
> Of all these ears (for where I am robb'd and bound,
> There must I be unloos'd, although not there
> At once and fully satisfied) whether ever I
> Did broach this business to your highness, or
> Laid any scruple in your way which might
> Induce you to the question on't.
>
> (II.iv.142)

Wolsey has been stung by Katherine's attacks on him as instigator of the whole affair, but his request to the king offers Henry the chance to take the reins into his own hands. Now, for the first time, he has a long, complicated and sturdy speech, in which he explains the origin of his desire for a divorce, and the motives that prompted him.[1] The motives are mixed, include the lack of an heir, and one he does not mention, Anne Boleyn, but it may be true too that he has been attempting, as he says:

> to rectify my conscience, which
> I then did feel full sick, and yet not well.
>
> (II.iv.203)

---

[1] Paul Bertram in '*Henry VIII*: The Conscience of the King', printed in *In Defence of Reason*, edited by Reuben Brower and Richard Poirier (New York, 1962), pp. 153-73, has argued that Henry's 'conscience speech is the turning point in the action', and that it prepares us to see 'Wolsey's role reduced to that of the mere ineffectual servant' (pp. 163-4).

The 'truth', as usual, is cloudy and hard to come at; but what this speech does dramatically is to establish Henry as King on his own, for the first time asserting himself, and not merely relying on others. It is ironical that Wolsey should prompt him to this, and nudge Henry into managing his own affairs. The king speaks no more to him in the scene, but leaps to the recognition that 'These cardinals trifle with me'.

From this point on he grows in strength as a character, a growth that reaches an appropriate climax in his relations with Cranmer in V.i. and V.ii. The archbishop, if Lovell, one of the commenting gentlemen can be trusted,

> Is the king's hand and tongue, and who dare speak
> One syllable against him?

(V.i.37)

He seems to have taken the place of Wolsey, but with the difference that Henry dominates from the beginning; Cranmer indeed enters to a frowning king:

> 'Tis his aspect of terror. All's not well.

(V.i.88)

He is simply fulfilling an appointment, and does not know that Henry is anxiously awaiting the birth of his child, and that his mind is far from business at this moment. Dramatically it gives the king an immediate ascendancy, which is maintained in his personal intervention in the council scene, where he appears as the careful sovereign watching over his ministers, the very reverse of his relations with Wolsey and Buckingham at the start of the play.

This emergence of Henry as ruler is part of the 'religious truth' of the play, overriding the contradictions, injustices and suffering that recur. The subtitle of *King Henry VIII*, 'All is True', relates to this, but also carries a powerful irony in reference to the truth in its more usual sense, that truth which is seen to be not accessible, except by accident, or through providence, to the observation of the characters, or to us in the audience. We are confronted with varieties of perspectives, and conflicting evidence, so that the whole truth about Buckingham, or Wolsey, or Henry, in their actions and motives always eludes us. Perhaps the final irony is that on this level it is Wolsey's words that are again fulfilled in the progress of Henry; for what he 'does worst' in divorcing Katherine, leads in the larger vision of 'religious truth' to the happiness of the realm through the birth of Elizabeth.

Index

184